# 1 MONTH OF
# FREE
# READING

## at

## www.ForgottenBooks.com

By purchasing this book you are eligible for one month membership to ForgottenBooks.com, giving you unlimited access to our entire collection of over 1,000,000 titles via our web site and mobile apps.

To claim your free month visit:

www.forgottenbooks.com/free200739

ISBN 978-0-265-19949-7
PIBN 10200739

PHILLIPS BIBLE INSTITUTE SERIES
of Efficiency Text-books for Bible Schools and Churches

# HOW TO BE SAVED

## A STUDY OF FIRST PRINCIPLES

By

## M. M. DAVIS, A.M.

Minister Ross Avenue Christian Church, Dallas, Tex.
Author of "Change of Heart;" "Queen Esther;"
"Elijah;" "First Principles;" "The Elder-
ship;" "The Restoration Movement of
the Nineteenth Century," and
"How the Disciples Began
and Grew."

CINCINNATI

.

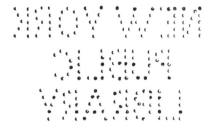

*To the Faculty and Student Body*
*of*
*Phillips Bible Institute*
*This Volume is Dedicated*
*by the Author*

# CONTENTS

IV.

## THE WISDOM AND PURITY OF CHRIST.

V.

## THE RESURRECTION OF CHRIST.

VI.

## FAITH.

VII.

## REPENTANCE.

Introductory—What is Repentance—It is Not Sorrow—It is Not Sorrow and Confession Combined—It is

## VIII.

## CONVERSION.

## IX.

## CHANGE OF HEART.

## X.

## THE CONFESSION.

## XI.

## BAPTISM.

## XII.

## EVIDENCE OF PARDON.

# FOREWORD

This book is both an abbreviation and expansion of the author's work on "First Principles." A considerable part of that volume is omitted, and much new matter is introduced, so that while the two are at many points the same, yet they are so different as to leave each a distinct and separate sphere of usefulness.

This change is because of a general desire for a book setting forth the distinctive features of the Restoration movement in a manner better fitted for use in colleges, efficiency church congresses and adult classes in the Bible school.

Hoping and praying for the blessings of the Father upon it, it is sent forth on its mission by

THE AUTHOR.

*Dallas, Texas.*

# I.
# IS THERE A GOD?

# OUTLINE—CHAPTER I.

**1.** INTRODUCTORY.
**2.** TWOFOLD ANSWER.
    *a.* ARGUMENT FROM WITHOUT.
    *b.* ARGUMENT FROM WITHIN.

**1. Introductory** A principle is a great mother truth containing m a n y other truths, or a fundamental law on which other laws rest, or from which they may be derived. "In all government truly republican," says Webster, "men are nothing—principle is everything." Let us therefore inquire as to what is the principle or princples which underlie, permeate and mould the life of the Christian. And in this inquiry we will not assume the "first principles," and begin far down the line of development, but our first inquiry shall be in regard to the existence of Him from whom every truly religious thought is derived, and in whom and on whom they must always abide: *"Is there a God?"*

The first questions in the heart of the intelligent and devout searcher after truth are not those relating to the commandments, ordinances and promises of the New Testament, but those concerning God. He goes back of all such questions as faith, repentance and baptism, and asks, "Is there a God? and, if so, how can I know him, and his will concerning me?"

A large volume might well be written in answer to these questions, and yet a helpful answer may be given in a small one. In fact, the answer must be condensed and simple or it can not reach the masses.

They have neither the time, the culture nor the inclination to read large and learned books. The wolf is at the door, and must be driven away, or the wife and little ones will go hungry. But they are willing and anxious to hear, and their hungry hearts are starving for knowledge, but it must not be stilted and stately, but primer-like, brief and simple.

But these people must not expect an absolutely perfect answer, for we know nothing with absolute perfection. We only know ourselves and our loved ones in part, and yet this partial knowledge is ample for present purposes. Bunyan's blind daughter never saw the face of her father, but she knew enough of him to love him, and bask in the many blessings which came from him. She felt his fond caresses; she heard his tender voice; and her life was sweetened and strengthened by his goodness and love. We are God's blind children. No man hath seen him at any time. But our faith, resting on indisputable evidence, has heard his message; and our consciences quickened by the message, and cleansed by the blood of Calvary, have received it; our hearts have been filled by his love; and our lives have been shaped by the teachings and example of the Saviour. Paul speaks of "that which *may be* known of God" (Rom. 1:19), implying that there was something which could not be known. The finite can not fully comprehend the infinite. The ocean can not be emptied into a teacup. If so, it would not be an ocean. The teacup may be filled from the ocean, but when filled it can contain no more until it is enlarged. And so we may **now** know God sufficiently well to believe in him, to love him and to serve him, but we must not expect to know him in his fullness. In the sweet by and by we shall know him *as he is,* but now we can only know him *as we are.* "When I was a child I spake as a child, I understood as a child, I thought as a child; but when I became a man I put away childish things. Now we see through a glass darkly, but then face to face; now I know in part, but then shall I know even as also I am known" (1 Cor. 13:11, 12).

**2. Twofold Answer**    *a.* ARGUMENT FROM WITHOUT. Every effect must not only have a cause, but it must have an adequate cause. This is an axiom. The simple statement carries conviction to all. A caravan was crossing a desert. An early riser reported that a camel had been walking about the tent during the night. He was asked how he knew it, and he pointed to the tracks in the sand, saying that nothing but a camel made such tracks. And when we look about us, we see the tracks of Jehovah. We see them in the hills and mountains; in the valleys and plains; in the rivers and oceans; in the flowers and trees; in the birds and fishes; in the sun, moon and stars; in the covenant of the day and night; in the coming and going of the seasons; and, most of all, in man himself. With all his splendid achievements —and they are splendid—man has not been able to make things like these. His mountains are mole-hills; his rivers are small canals; his oceans are toy lakes; his flowers are without life or fragrance, and

2

his lights are flickering tapers. Napoleon, not only the greatest soldier of his age, but also one of the world's wisest philosophers, with some of his officers, was on his way to Egypt. The night was clear, the sea was calm, and the sky above the ship was studded with stars. The officers were engaged in an animated religious discussion, and when it was about to close they seemed to have proven to their own satisfaction that there was no God. Their hero all the while was apparently absorbed in other things, but it was only in appearance. He had heard the entire discussion, and had noted their conclusion, for, just as it closed, he said to them, "All that is very well, gentlemen;" and, pointing to the myriads of stars blazing in glory above them, he asked, "but who made these?" Echo answers, "Who?" They are the tracks of Jehovah. "The heavens declare the glory of God, and the firmament showeth the work of his hands" (Ps. 19:1).

Design, like the argument from cause and effect, is old, simple and sound. It can never be overturned. We might as well expect to see the rocks of Gibraltar hurled into the sea as to look for a successful refutation of this great argument. An intelligent man for the first time examines an ordinary watch, with its complicated and intricate machinery. He notes its levers and springs, its wheels and cogs, its strong case and clear face, its hour, minute and second hands, and he sees how accurately it marks the progress of time. What must be his conclusion? Please note that I do not ask what it *may be,* but what it *must be.* There can be but one: This watch had a designer; it could not have come by chance. Dr. Franklin once silenced a skeptic on this wise. The skeptic argued that the world did not imply a designer, but that it was the result of chance. One morning when this skeptical friend called, Franklin showed him a small globe. He had never seen one before, and asked what it was, and who made it. Franklin told him that it was a picture of the earth, but no one made it; it just happened to be in that shape; it was a freak of chance. His friend saw the point, and his skepticism vanished. And I would ask, Which is the easier—to make the globe, or to make its picture?

If you should visit a new country and find palaces, gardens, streets, railways, steamships, and all things necessary for the comfort of man, could you fail to believe that these things were the result of design? With the alphabet in a sack, would you expect to shake it up and pour it on paper and get a poem? With the colors thrown carelessly on the canvas, would you expect a picture? Is it not as reasonable to believe that the palaces of the world came by chance as that this splendid earthly home of ours so came? If even a little poem must have an intelligent author, how can we believe the great volume of nature has none? Why not a painting by chance as well as this marvelous picture gallery of the universe? Is it easier to make a man than to make his picture?

If you should see a ship making annual voyages to some distant port, and returning at a regular time, laden with food and clothing for the people of an isolated island, and never deviating a mile from her course, and never an hour late, would it be possible to believe it the result of chance? Although you never saw them, still you would know she had a captain, a pilot, a chart and compass, who directed her on her missions of mercy. Let us think of our world as a great ship sweeping round the sun, and returning laden with all that man needs, and never out of her course the fraction of an inch, or a single second late. It must be that a wise and loving Father is at the helm. Reason as well as revelation can accept no other conclusion.

Joseph Cook finds in nature a beautiful illustration of this thought. He says that almost imperceptible creatures are building, in the Indian Ocean, a vessel known as "Neptune's Cup." It is sometimes six feet high, and half as broad. These little creatures have no consultation with each other. Each works in a separate cell, cut off from the other, like prisoners in a penitentiary. They build the stem to the proper height, and then begin to widen. Everything is proportioned according to a perfect plan. Is the plan theirs? or does it proceed from a power above them and act through them? So the bioplasts, isolated from each other in the living tissues which they produce, build the rose and violet and all flowers; the pomegranate, cedar, oak and all trees; the eagle, canary and all birds; the lion, leopard and all animals; the bone, muscle and all men; and so from the cup he drank the glad wine of design.

*b.* ARGUMENT FROM WITHIN. The heavens and the earth, with all creation, proclaim the presence and power of God. This is wonderful testimony, and constitutes a foundation on which the soundest reason and profoundest philosophy may rear the Temple of Hope. But it is not all, nor is it the best. God would have his children without excuse in this matter of faith, and hence he makes the voice within corroborate that from without, and thus the basis of the religious life is made doubly sure.

God makes no half hinges. The desire on the part of man for bread, water, light and sound presupposes his capacity for, and his need of, these things, just as the fin of the fish implies a fluid in which to swim, and the wing of the bird an atmosphere in which to fly. The Being who created the bird and fish also created these elements, and without them they could not exist. The Creator of man so constituted him that he must have bread and water, or he will die; and he must have light and sound in order to attain the highest physical life. These things are part and parcel of his fleshly life, and in his normal condition they are never absent. All men, believers and unbelievers alike, agree here. And they agree, further, that these wants are not the result of teaching or development, but are a part of his nature.

Can we find a parallel of this in his spiritual nature? If so, then it follows with the force of a demonstration that there is a God. Man has been called a "religious animal." He has been characterized as "hopelessly so"; i. e., he is not only religious by nature, but his religious instincts can not be destroyed. He has never been discovered without

some form of religion. However fallen and degraded, there is something within which reaches
after God; and a piteous voice that cries to the
unseen for help. A few times he has been found so
low that at first it was thought he had no spiritual
aspirations. But, on closer examination, this was
discovered to be an error. It is as easy to find him
without speech as without religion. It is a part of
his very being, and his soul can no more exist without it than his body can live without bread and water.
William Shakespeare, the world's great poet, it is
supposed knew something of human nature; and
here is what he says on this point:

> "The dread of something after death,
>   That undiscovered country
>   From whose bourne no traveler returns,
>   Puzzles the will. . . .
>   *Thus* conscience doth make cowards of us all."

Put emphasis on "thus," and you get the poet's
point. Looking forward to a place of punishment
beyond the veil makes cowards of us all. Not simply
such as are under the influence of Christianity, but
also the ancient Greek, Roman and pagan. This
dread is a part of our nature, and is as natural as
the song in the moment of joy, and the groan in the
moment of sorrow. It is organic and ineradicable.
And this is not simply the teaching of Shakespeare,
but is the voice of the great students of human
nature since time began. And it is also the voice
of Paul. "When the Gentiles, which have not the
law, do by nature the things contained in the law,
these, having not the law, are a law unto themselves;

which show the work of the law written in their hearts, their conscience also bearing witness, and their thoughts the meanwhile accusing or else excusing one another" (Rom. 2:14, 15). Bishop Butler says: "Conscience without being consulted, always naturally, and of course, unless forcibly stopped, goes forward to anticipate a sentence higher than its own, and which shall hereafter second and confirm its decisions." It is this which is so large an element in our own desire for God, and it must be accounted for. A volcanic peak suddenly rises a thousand feet above the water in midocean. What is its basis? No sane man would say that it rested on the waves. There must be something solid beneath it. But such a towering peak would not be more prominent than this instinctive propensity of man to worship. On what does it rest? It is deep-seated, and refuses to be removed. He may be induced to abandon an old religion and espouse a new one, but he must have religion. If he loses knowledge of the true God, he will adopt a false one. There is no pinnacle in the whole range of human nature which stands out more clearly than this; and therefore it must rest on the same basis which supports human nature.

A student was annoyed by the singing of a canary. Some one suggested that it was a bird in another cage which made it sing, and he moved it. But the song continued. It was not the presence of its companion which made it sing, but a something within, placed there by its Maker. Its song was a part of its life—as much so as shining is a part of the life of the sun, and as exhaling fragrance is a part of the life of the rose; and so, whether alone or with its companion, in shine or shade, in winter and in summer, always and everywhere the canary sings. So the heart sings to God, not because of the absence or presence of friends or foes, or because of any outside influence, but because of its innate yearnings. Beecher says: "The ocean is the same, whatever craft sail up and down upon it; whether they be pleasure-boats, brigs, or merchant-ships, pirates or men-of-war; so, whatever religious navigators may be going up and down the sea of life, its depths and shores and distant haven remain the same. The stars never change for astrologers or astronomers. They roll calmly above storms and above opinions. So man's nature does not vary for circumstances or conflicting views, but still wants God above, and fellow-man below."

It is as impossible for us to get away from God as it was when David wrote: "Whither shall I go from thy spirit? or whither shall I flee from thy presence? If I ascend up into heaven, thou art there: if I make my bed in the grave, behold, thou art there. If I take the wings of the morning, and dwell in the uttermost parts of the sea; even there shall thy hand lead me, and thy right hand shall hold me. If I say, Surely the darkness shall cover me; even the night shall be light about me. Yea, the darkness hideth not from thee; but the night shineth as the day: the darkness and the light are both alike to thee" (Ps. 139: 7-12). He follows us as the shadow follows the substance. This thought was powerfully impressed on me the day I first saw Pike's Peak, the great monarch of the Rockies, standing like a sentinel from the skies, guarding that world of mountains. I needed no one to point it out to me. The moment my eyes rested on it, I exclaimed, "There's Pike's Peak!" And for almost a hundred miles it was seldom out of view, and seemed to keep alongside of our train, as if it, too, was moving. It looked as if we would never get away from it. And so the thought of God, towering high above all others, follows us through every experience in life. It fills the mind of the little child with awe, and trembles in reverence on the lips of old age. It throbs in the heart of youth as he nears manhood, and becomes his inspiration in the stern battles of life. It is a benediction at the marriage altar, and the one solace and stay at the open grave. It goes side by side with the poor wretch on the downward way to ruin, and on the pathway of the just it shines more and more unto the perfect day. The murderer can not drive it from his narrow cell, and all bad men and demons combined can not rob the dying martyr of its holy presence. And during eternity it will still soothe the soul.

Tell man that there is no God, and after a moment of terrible suspense he will look you in the face and declare that your teaching is inhuman; that if this life is not to be followed by another and better life; that if hopes are only born to be blighted; if ties are only made to be sundered; if heart yearnings are only roused to be crushed; if man is only created to be destroyed—then God must be either

weak or wicked.    He will quote you Browning's
forceful lines:

> "Truly there needs another life to come!
> If this be all,
> And another life await us not, for one,
> I say 'tis a poor cheat, a stupid bungle,
> A wretched failure.  I for one protest
> Against, and I hurl it back with scorn."

Is there a God?    Yes; or the voice of Nature is
false, and the deepest instincts of the heart are mis-
leading.

### REVIEW.

1. Define "principle."

2. What is the **first** question in the heart of a
truth-seeker?

3. May we expect perfect answers?

4. Give the first argument.

5. Give the second argument.

6. Give the Dr. Franklin incident.

7. Give the illustrations of the poem, picture
**and** watch.

8. Tell us of "Neptune's Cup."

9. Give the argument from "within."

10. Is worship natural to man?

# II.

# GOD SPEAKING TO HIS CHILDREN

# OUTLINE—CHAPTER II.

1. UNITY.
   a. THE PEOPLE FROM WHOM IT CAME.
   b. THE NUMBER OF WRITERS.
   c. CHARACTER OF WRITERS.
   d. LENGTH OF TIME THEY WERE WRITING.
   e. CHANGES DURING THIS TIME.
2. VITALITY.
   a. SOME ARE COMMONPLACE.
   b. SOME ARE DISPLACED BY BETTER BOOKS.
   c. SOME ARE FALSE.
3. UTILITY.
   a. GEOGRAPHICAL.
   b. LAW.
   c. POLITICS.
   d. LITERATURE.
   e. PAINTING.
   f. SCULPTURE.
   g. MUSIC.
   h. WOMAN.
4. ADAPTATION.
5. INDESTRUCTIBILITY.
6. PROGRESSIVENESS.
7. REVELATIONS.

# II.

## God Speaking to His Children.

If there is a God, and if that God, as the Christian believes, is our Father, then we may be sure he has spoken to his children; for what earthly parent, with a child away from home, would not, if he could, communicate with him? Hence our second study: *Did the Bible come from God?*

In the discussion of this large question both our purpose and space forbid the discussion of details. Even the much-discussed question of inspiration must be passed by with a sentence, for we have in mind the young soul in search of the truth, and not the learned theologian, or the average Christian with years of experience and knowledge. Lowth, speaking on this subject, says: "Inspiration may be regarded, not as suppressing or extinguishing for a time the faculties of the human mind, but of purifying and strengthening and elevating them above what they would otherwise reach." It is like the sun shining through colored glass. The colors in the glass are not destroyed, but rather heightened and brightened. And so the personality of the Bible writers is preserved and perpetuated. Paul, for example, is as distinctly himself when inspired by God, as when he writes of his own accord.

Nature bears the marks of divine origin. Man never made the heavens or the earth. As well might we say that the great bridges which span our rivers and the ships which ride the seas are the works of ten-year-old boys. And so the Bible bears marks of its divine origin. What are some of them?

**1. Its Unity** The Bible is one book; not because it is bound in a single voulme, but because of the plan and purpose manifest on every page. "Paradise Lost" and "The Course of Time" are not more distinct unities. Barnes is right in claiming that it has "a beginning, a middle and an end—a beginning, a middle and an end more complete, extending through more years, and embracing a greater variety of characters and events, than any other volume in the world—its beginning the beginning of creation; its middle the Incarnation and the Atonement; its end the consummation of the world's affairs."

That we may the better appreciate this high and true claim, let us remember:

*a.* THE PEOPLE FROM WHOM IT CAME. The Jews had no scientific or literary fame. They were regarded as narrow and bigoted, with no ambition in these directions. The Chaldeans and Egyptians had their observatories through which they were familiar with the heavens, and splendid temples dedicated to literature, science and religion. Had the Bible come from these people, it would not have been so strange. But it came from a people just the reverse; a people as incapable of producing such a book, as Alaska is of producing the California orange. And yet Milton (and who knows better?) says: "No songs are comparable to the songs of

Zion; no orations are equal to those of the prophets; and no politics are like those which the Scriptures teach."

*b.* THE NUMBER OF THE WRITERS. The Bible of the Chinese has but one author—Confucius; and the Koran is from the pen of Mohammed. But the Bible has about forty authors.

*c.* CHARACTER OF THESE WRITERS. Some of them were men of renown, and others were fishermen and shepherds. Some were men of culture, and others were "unlearned and ignorant." Some of them, by travel, had come in touch with the wisdom of the world, but most of them were never beyond the narrow limits of their native land. Travel, a vital factor in education, was denied them.

*d.* THE LENGTH OF TIME THEY WERE WRITING. The Bible was not written in a single year, or during a period of several years, but more than fifteen hundred years swept by between its beginning and its close.

*e.* THE CHANGES GOING ON IN THE WORLD DURING THIS TIME. These were many and vast. The whole earth was feverish and restive like a volcano; it heaved and sighed and groaned like an ocean in a storm. Great conquerors founded empires which swayed the world for a moment, and then passed away; and discoveries followed each other in rapid succession in the scientific world; there was as little rest among the scholars as among the soldiers; and vast revolutions of many kinds were shaking the earth to her center. But, despite all this, the Bible writers, like men in a cave, sheltered from the storm raging about them, slowly and surely pushed their work to completion.

How, under these circumstances, are we to account for the perfect unity of the Bible? It came from a people who had never produced anything of the kind; it is the joint work of more than forty writers differing greatly from each other and without conference with each other, or knowledge of the fact that they were engaged in writing a single book; their work covered a period of more than fifteen hundred years of the most turbulent history of the world. (What man has lived long enough to supervise the writing of a book during so long a time?) And yet the keynote sounded at first was the keynote to the last. "It is susceptible of easy proof," says Barnes, "that one part is the completion or complement of the other, as the two parts of a tally, or as complementary colors; not as the Jews would have done it, but as it was intended to be. There is a scheme commenced. There is an anticipation. There is progress. There is a completion in the Messiah. There is the unfolding of a plan through many centuries; one writer in one age stating one thing, and another in another, as if in one age an artist should have fashioned an arm, and another a leg, and one a hand and another a foot; one the nose, another the lips, another the chin; one the form and size of the head, and another the body; and all at last should have been put together in the form of Minerva or Apollo." Such a book is as different from all other books as the sun is different from a taper, and, like the sun, it bears on its shining face the proof of its divine origin.

**2. Its Vitality**  Books, like men, are born, live their little day, die, and are forgotten. This results from various causes:

*a*. THEY ARE COMMONPLACE. They lack the merit that perpetuates. They have a few friends and a local reputation, but the great, wide world neither knows of them nor cares for them. It is appalling to see this large and ever-increasing list; it is enough to make an author's pen fall from his fingers. It is like the advance of an army, which can be traced by the refuse in its wake. Here is an old wagon; there is a disabled piece of artillery; and yonder an old horse, no longer able to keep his place in the ranks. And so there are many books which can not keep up with the procession of this ongoing world. Their only friend is the antiquarian. We may preserve them because they are rare. But this is a doubtful honor, for if they had been valuable they would not have been rare.

*b*. THEY HAVE BEEN DISPLACED BY BETTER BOOKS. If all of this class were piled together, they would make a small mountain. They were once useful, but better books have taken their place, and they are now fit companions of the old-time engine and reaper.

*c*. THEY ARE FALSE. The works of Ptolemy, with all other books founded on the Ptolemaic system of astronomy, are illustrations of this class. Though ingenious and profound, they passed away

3

when the Copernican theory was established; and their chief value to-day is that they mark the mighty progress of science.

But the Bible belongs to none of these classes. It is not found in the hands of the antiquarian, honored solely because of its quaintness and its age; better books are not pushing it aside and it is not being discarded because of its errors; but it holds its high place in the vanguard of the world. It is translated into more languages than any other book; better presses are printing it; more money and skill are spent on its embellishment; it finds a welcome in more and better homes; and its influence is now greater than ever before. It has withstood alike its furious foes and its false friends; and, like its Author, it remains the same "yesterday, to-day and for ever," needing no revision and adaptation, as does our Constitution. A few years ago, when a new translation of the New Testament reached New York, a Chicago daily, rather than wait a few hours for the railroad train to bring it, had it flashed over the wires, and gave it in full in a single issue to its readers. Does that look like it had lost vitality? It throbs with life to-day as it has always done, and it thrills with life everything that receives it. It is as unlike any other book as the mountain is like a molehill, and it shows, as does the mountain, that Jehovah is its Author.

**3. Its Utility** Here is, perhaps, its highest proof of heavenly origin. That which always ennobles, elevates and purifies must be of God. In my old Virginia home the land is thin and much fertilizer is used, each plant of tobacco receiving a tablespoonful of the guano. It sometimes happens that a small part of a field is neglected because the supply of fertilizer is exhausted. In such a case you can tell by the feebleness of the plant every one so neglected. And when we look over the world we can discover by the rich foliage and fruit just where the fertilizing influence of the old Book has gone. "Where there is no vision, the people perish: but he that keepeth the law, happy is he" (Prov. 29:18).

There are those who claim that human culture, philosophy, science, art, etc., are better for man than the Bible. If so, the map of the world should show it. Egypt was once the seat of the world's best learning, but her scholars as well as her serfs bowed in worship to the brute. Greece in her palmiest days, when reason and philosophy reigned supreme, was gross and sensual in her devotions. And when Corinth was famous for beauty and elegance, Venus, the very personification of lust, was her goddess. At best these powers could only elevate the few, and these they failed to purify. They could build the pyramids and the Coliseum, but they could not build up the morals of the people. One emperor slew twenty thousand men in celebrating a Roman holiday.

*a.* GEOGRAPHICAL. Now see the Bible tested. Look upon the lands where it has been open to the masses, and you see the noblest men, the purest women, the largest liberty and the best government. Behold England, Scotland and America. Then follow the missionary in Asia, Africa and the Sandwich Islands, and see vice changed to virtue; savages to saints; barbarism to civilization; and woman, the degraded beast of burden, loved and honored as mother, wife, sister and daughter. Some years since a ship was wrecked off one of the Fiji Islands. The crew expected to be devoured by cannibals. But when two of them discovered a church, they shouted, "All right; here is a church; no fear now!"

*b.* LAW. And in its influence it touches all parts of life. In the realm of law, reason perhaps reaches its highest development, and yet the Bible seems a fixture there. A skeptical lawyer, impressed with the accuracy, profundity and marvelous comprehensiveness of the Ten Commandments, said: "I have read history. The Egyptians and the adjacent nations were idolaters; so were the Greeks and Romans; and the wisest and best Greeks and Romans never gave a code like this. Where did Moses get this law which surpasses the wisdom and philosophy of the most enlightened ages?" And soon he became a Christian. And along with this sound reasoner are found Blackstone, Marshall, Story and Kent.

*c.* POLITICS. It also blesses in the political realm. Even Voltaire said, "Not to believe in any God would be an error incompatible with wise government." An African prince sent an ambassador to Queen Victoria, asking the secret of England's superiority among the nations. The Queen, handing the ambassador a copy of the Bible, said, "Go tell your prince that this is the secret of England's political greatness." And Japan was unknown as a world power until the Book was opened in her midst. The nation that receives it feels the flush of health and the vigor of life in the body politic. Great statesmen like Burke and Pitt and Webster might be called as witnesses here. Let us hear Webster: "If we abide by the principles taught in the Bible, our country will go on prospering and to prosper, but if we and our posterity neglect its instructions and authority, no man can tell how sudden a catastrophe may overwhelm us, and bury our glory in obscurity."

*d*. LITERATURE. And what is true in law and political science is equally true in learning and literature. Whence the origin of the great schools of the civilized world, such as Prague, Heidelberg, Leipzig, Cambridge, Oxford, Harvard and Yale?

Now, is it strange that in this realm it makes and moulds the best, for when mind meets mind, both are sharpened; and when the mind of man comes in contact with the mind of God, every human faculty is aroused to the utmost. When blind Bunyan was locked up for twelve years in Bedford jail, his library consisted of the Bible and Fox's "Book of Martyrs," and he produced "Pilgrim's Progress," the most remarkable book of its kind in the world. And Shakespeare, that wonderful prodigy, who, like the sun, belongs to all men, would not have been Shakespeare but for the Bible. His works contain more than five hundred Bible quotations and Bible sentiments. He quotes from or refers to fifty-four of its sixty-six books; and in every one of his thirty-seven plays there are Scriptural references. These two masterpieces in literature, like most of the best things in it, are saturated with the word of God.

*e.* PAINTING. And what would the world of painting be without the Bible? There would be no Raphael's "Transfiguration"; no Angelo's "Last Judgment"; no Murillo's "Moses Striking the Rock"; no Rubens' "Descent from the Cross," and no Da Vinci's "Last Supper."

*f.* SCULPTURE. In sculpture, a sister to the realm of painting, the loss would be equally great. We would miss Angelo's "Moses"; Canova's "Penitent Magdalene," and Thorwaldsen's "Christ and the Apostles."

*g.* MUSIC. Without this Book the world of music would be poor indeed. We would not have Handel's "Sampson," "Saul" and "Messiah"; nor Haydn's "Creation"; nor Beethoven's "Mount of Olives"; nor Mendelssohn's "Elijah" and "Paul."

*h.* WOMAN. And what would woman be without this blessed Book? Before its gracious beams shone upon her way, she was the toy or plaything of man, or a beast of burden yoked with the oxen of the field. Even in the classic glory of Greece the most common symbol on her tomb was a muzzle, implying that she should not speak; or a pair of reins, indicating that she should be driven by her husband. But, with its aid, she has risen to the high, holy and tender place of mother, wife, sister and daughter.

But what need to say more? What it has done in these spheres, it has done in all spheres. It blesses all ranks and conditions—the rich and the poor, the weak and the strong, the wise and the ignorant, the master and the slave, the prince and the peasant.

And its blessings are not confined to the spiritual. It builds schoolhouses, colleges and universities, as we have already seen; it builds hospitals, almshouses and orphanages; it builds railroads, telegraphs and steamships. In a word, it gives to us our best civilization, and, as the benediction of Heaven, it ever hovers over the home of man.

In proof of all this let us hear a single famous witness, and one whose bias was against the Book— Charles Darwin. While on a scientific voyage he touched at Terre del Fuego. He was horrified at the degradation of the inhabitants, and doubted whether they belonged to the human race. Science noted the awful fact, but made no effort to change it; but the church, hearing the sad news, rushed to the rescue. Two noble fellows led the way, and were murdered by the bloodthirsty savages. But again and again the ranks of the fallen were refilled, until the victory of the Cross was won. And, let it be said in honor of Mr. Darwin, when he saw what the Bible had done for them, he became a regular contributor to the South American Missionary Society.

**4. Its Adaptation** There are to-day one billion five hundred thousand people on the earth, and they are as varied as the leaves of the forest or the grasses of the field—the white man, the black man, the yellow man, the brown man—and yet this Book, when its teachings are heard and heeded, meets all the spiritual wants of this vast throng. No man can deny the race distinctions among them, for they are as clear as the distinctions between the lion, the horse and the ox. Yet it is the glory of the

Book that it has a voice for every race, and a helping hand for every man. At a meeting in Glasgow this question was being discussed, when one speaker argued that some races, like the Bushman, were so degraded as to be beyond the reach of the Bible. A stranger rose and said: "I don't pretend to be able to dispute with the learned gentleman, but I will tell what I know, for I am a Bushman, one of the same little fellows he claims are incapable of moral development  One of them was educated and converted by a missionary. One night an English cavalry officer was lost. Filled with despair, he saw a light in the distance. The Bushman, hearing the clatter of the horse's feet, stood in the door of his humble home, and, at the approach of the lost soldier, he bowed low, and asked him to come in. When supper was over and bedtime came, he told the stranger that it was the custom in that home to read the Bible and pray before going to sleep, and he requested the Englishman to lead in that service. But he said with shamefacedness that he had never learned to pray. The Bushman himself then read and prayed. In the light of this example I think it clear that even this stunted, jabbering, ape-like race is capable of receiving and living the truth of God."

**5. Its Indestructibility**  No book ever had such firm friends and such furious foes as the Bible. The war waged against it has been bitter, long and relentless; but, like the burning bush, it refuses to be consumed. Critics in all ages, learned and strong, have shown to their own satisfaction that it was a myth or a fable, unworthy

of God, and unfit for man.  A hundred years ago
it was outlawed in France, and the awful Reign of
Terror began.  The Bible was burned, God was
dethroned, the Lord's Day was erased from the stat-
ute-books, and the streets of Paris ran with blood.
It looked like all was lost.  Voltaire, the leader, bold
and blatant, said: "I am going through the forests
of your Christian doctrines, and will girdle every
tree, so that presently not a sapling shall be left
you."  (Little did he think that the very house used
by him in which to declare his purpose and print
his prophecy would soon become a depository for
the Bible and other religious literature.)  Unbelief,
like a great dark cloud, seemed to be settling down
over Europe, and smothering out the last ray of
light.  Nor was it confined to Europe.  It swept
across the Atlantic and invaded America.  Tom
Paine published his "Age of Reason," and the
effect was frightful.  He showed the manuscript to
Benjamin Franklin, who urged him not to "unloose
this tiger," saying: "If our people are only what
they are with the Bible, what would they be without
it?"  But he did unloose it, and for a time it seemed
that Paine's book, and not God's, was to rule in our
beloved land.

And the fight is still on, but the method of war-
fare is changed.  The attack from without has given
place to one from within.  The great leaders of open
infidelity are gone.  Bradlaugh in Europe and Inger-
soll in America closed the battle on that line.  But
the struggle continues.  The leaders are often robed
in the garbs of Christian teachers, preachers, authors

and editors. Like the enemies of Troy who came into the city in the wooden horse, they are striving to open the gates from within.

But what is the result? The old Book stands. It emerges from the furnace of every foe, though heated seven times hot, without the smell of fire on its garments, or the loss of a single vital doctrine. It stands like Gibraltar, with the wreck of many hostile fleets floating at its base. The assaults from the open foe have not breached its walls, nor have its bolts been drawn by treachery within.

**6. Its Progressiveness** The coming and going of the nations is the drama of all dramas. The Babylonian, Egyptian, Persian and other great powers have lived their little day and died. Great discoveries and wonderful inventions have followed each other in rapid succession. Scientific and philosophical theories have changed and rechanged, and laws have been enacted and remodeled so as to meet the wants of a growing world. But the Bible has kept pace with every forward movement, and is still as perfectly adapted to the wants of the world as it was when it first came from the hand of God. *Progress is fatal to a falsehood, but to the truth it is its best tonic.*

We outgrow many things—our text-books, our schools, our habits, our pleasures; but no one can outgrow the Bible. We may grow away from it, but none have outgrown it. We find room within its ample scope for continuous growth in everything that is good. And when we turn from it we are dwarfed.

**7. Its Revelations** Its practical precepts are the best in the world. Its principles are without a flaw. Its influence is always good. But, passing on beyond the questions of daily life and duty, it deals with problems untouched by other books. It tells us of the origin and destiny of man. It solves the soul's greatest questions. Other books leave man at the grave without hope, and his going from the earth is a leap in the dark. But this Book tells the Christian that death is a transition from the lower to the higher, from the imperfect to the perfect. The grave is the robing-room in which the soul is dressed for an audience with the Lord of lords and the King of kings.

Whence, then, this wonderful Book? How came it with a unity as perfect as that of the human body? How came it with a vitality which ignores the passage of time, and though old in years, like its Lord, still retains the dew of its youth? How came it with the magic power that blesses everything it touches? How came it to be perfectly adapted to all men in all places and in every condition? Why is it that it refuses to be destroyed, and defies the might and malice of every foe? Why is it that it moves in the vanguard of a growing world and constantly taunts its enemies by saying: "Supplement me; supersede me; supplant me, if you can!" Whence its power to take away the sting of death, to light up the dark vault of the grave, to unbolt the gates of the New Jerusalem and usher the soul into the presence of its Maker and Redeemer? Well has Alfred M. Haggard said: "I know that no man made the roses. I know that no man painted the sunset on the evening skies. In the same way I know that no man, nor set of men, unaided, have produced the Bible. It points to God as its Author as do the flowers and the sunset skies."

Columbus never explored South America, but only touched a few places on the northern coast, and yet he unhesitatingly pronounced it a continent. As he gazed on the vast volume of fresh water rushing through the wide-mouthed Orinoco into the sea, he said: "That stream, comrades, never came from an island; be sure it gathered its vast waters from a continent." And when we contemplate the influences flowing from this matchless Book, we instinctively exclaim: "It came not from man, but from man's Maker!"

## REVIEW.

1. Is revelation reasonable?
2. What of the unity of the Bible?
3. What of the vitality of the Bible?
4. What of the utility of the Bible?
5. What of the adaptation of the Bible?
6. What of the indestructibility of the Bible?
7. What of the progressiveness of the Bible?
8. Give the quotation from Haggard.
9. Give the illustration by Columbus.

# III.

# HOW TO STUDY THE NEW TESTAMENT

# OUTLINE—CHAPTER III.

1. FIRST WANT.
   a. BAPTISM OF JESUS.
   b. CALMING THE STORM.
   c. FEEDING THE MULTITUDE.
   d. RAISING OF LAZARUS.
2. SECOND WANT.
   a. THE UNBELIEVER.
   b. THE BELIEVER.
   c. THE PENITENT BELIEVER.
   d. THE BACKSLIDER.
3. THIRD WANT.
4. FOURTH WANT.

# III.

## How to Study the New Testament.

The whole Bible is from God, and therefore it should be faithfully studied by his children. But there are special reasons why we should study the New Testament. It is the Father's latest and fullest revelation, including the Gentile as well as the Jew, and giving us, in fact, what the Old Testament gives in picture and in promise. It is the constitution of the new covenant under which we live, and a full knowledge of this covenant can not be had except through the New Testament. Much injury has resulted from the want of a clean-cut distinction between the Old and New Testaments. Many religious teachers treat the two volumes as if they were identical in their teachings. They are as apt to send a penitent sinner to the Psalms of David or the wailings of Jeremiah for instruction as to how to be saved, as to the Book of Acts. And when we come to the New Testament we often find similar confusion. They seem to think that the different parts of the book just happened to get into their present places; that Matthew might as well have been the last book as the first and that Revelation was not necessarily the last section of the volume. The idea, in many cases, seems to be that these different books of the New Testament found their several places much as different tracts might find

45

theirs, when bound together by a publisher without reference to their contents. But such a conception is as far from the truth as the east is from the west. This book is as systematic in its arrangement as any text-book. Matthew is first because it ought to be first, and Revelation is last because it ought to be last, and so of every other book.

Man, spiritually, is a fourfold creature, and the book is fourfold in its divisions, each division meeting the spiritual wants in the order of their occurrence. These divisions have each one great fundamental purpose which gives character to them. It is true they contain many other important things, but these are subordinate. The Mississippi River, in its long journey, runs toward every point of the compass; therefore, it might be truthfully said that it flows east, west, north and south; and yet, when speaking in general, it is correct to say that it flows southward because this is its main course.

1. First Want    The first spiritual want of one studying Christianity relates to Christ. An educated Hindoo, with a clear head and good heart, having heard of the Christian religion, lands in New York for the purpose of investigating it. The first Sunday morning finds him listening to a Presbyterian preacher. When he analyzes the sermon he finds that its central thought is that of a great person called by various names: Christ, Jesus, Saviour, Lord, etc. At night he hears a Methodist preacher, whose sermon in many respects is different from the other, but both are identical so far as this central thought is concerned. He continues to hear

eminent men for months, and they differ in a thousand minor details, but are a unit concerning the Christ. He is to their theology what the sun is to the solar system—its center; the point around which all things else revolve, and from which they receive their light and life. He now selects a competent teacher, and his studies begin in earnest.

This teacher, that this first want of his may be supplied, directs him in a careful study of the first division of the New Testament: Matthew, Mark, Luke and John. He has him witness the baptism of Jesus, with the visible dovelike descent of the Spirit, and the audible voice from the skies.

*a.* BAPTISM OF JESUS. "Then cometh Jesus from Galilee to Jordan to be baptized of John. But John forbade him, saying, I have need to be baptized of thee, and comest thou to me? And Jesus answering said unto him, Suffer it to be so now, for thus it becometh us to fulfil all righteousness. Then he suffered him. And Jesus, when he was baptized, went up straightway out of the water, and lo, the heavens were opened unto him, and he saw the Spirit of God descending like a dove, and lighting upon him. And lo, a voice from heaven, saying, This is my beloved Son, in whom I am well pleased" (Matt. 3: 13-17).

His pupil is deeply impressed, and asks for further instruction.

*b.* CALMING THE STORM. He is next shown the Lord as he hushes the sea into silence. "And the same day, when the evening was come, he said unto them, Let us pass over unto the other side. And when they had sent away the multitude, they took him even as he was in the ship. . . . And there arose a great storm of wind, and the waves beat into the ship, so that it was now full. And he was in the hinder part of the ship asleep on a pillow; and they awoke him, and say unto him, Master, carest thou not that we perish? And he arose and rebuked the wind, and said unto the sea, Peace, be still. And the wind ceased, and there was a great calm" (Mark 4:35-39).

The tired Saviour is asleep in the little boat. The storm-king arouses the waves and the sea becomes so furious that the disciples, experienced seamen, familiar with such dangers, moved with fear, awoke him, saying, "Master, carest thou not that we perish?" Arising from his hard bed, filled with the majesty and mercy of Jehovah, he waves his hand and says, "Peace, be still!" and the wild winds cease their roaring, the mad waves crouch at his feet, and the sea, calm as an infant's slumber, permits the frail vessel to pass on in safety to the shore. The teacher asks what he thinks of One whom the winds and the waves obey. He answers, "He is wonderful; but let me see more of him."

*c*. FEEDING THE MULTITUDE. They now go to a desert place to see him feed the five thousand on five loaves and two fishes. "When Jesus heard of it [the death of John] he departed thence by ship into a desert place apart; and when the people had heard thereof, they followed him on foot out of the cities. And Jesus went forth, and saw a great multitude, and was moved with compassion toward them, and he healed their sick. And when it was evening, his disciples came to him, saying, This is a desert place, and the time is now past; send the multitude away, that they may go into the villages, and buy themselves victuals. But Jesus said unto them, They need not depart; give ye them to eat. And they say unto him, We have here but five loaves and two fishes. He said, Bring them hither to me. And he commanded the multitude to sit down on the grass, and took the five loaves, and the two fishes, and looking up to heaven, he blessed, and brake, and gave the loaves to his disciples, and the disciples to the multitude. And they did all eat, and were filled: and they took up of the fragments that remained twelve baskets full. And they that had eaten were about five thousand men, besides women and children" (Matt. 14: 13-21).

The young Hindoo witnesses this remarkable scene with great astonishment and awe. He sees the hungry throng of five thousand men, with probably as many more women and children—ten thousand in all—seated on the soft grass; he sees the little pittance of food brought to Jesus; he beholds him looking up to God, and hears his strange, sweet voice as he blesses it; he then watches him as he gives it to the disciples, and they to the multitude; and he notices how these starving people devour it. And when all are fed, he is astonished to find that more food remains that they had in the beginning.

Again the teacher seeks an opinion, and again his pupil expresses wonder, but asks for more evidence before rendering a verdict.

Before leaving this miracle, let me say that it is one of the greatest the Saviour ever wrought. It is easy to deceive the eye, the ear and the touch; but not so of the appetite of a hungry man. You can not convince him that he has been fed until you feed him. If you think you can, try it with the hungry schoolboy, as he comes bounding home from school. And yet Jesus, with these few loaves and fishes, convinced these hungry thousands that they had been fed.

*d.* RAISING OF LAZARUS. The resurrection of Lazarus (John 11: 1-46) is next studied. The Christ, with the sympathy of a man and the power of God, cries with a loud voice, "Lazarus, come forth!" And the arms of Death are broken, and the dead, alive again, is restored to his weeping sisters. Doubt now vanishes, and the young man joyfully proclaims: "It is enough! It is enough! I believe in Jesus as the Son of God and the Saviour of men!"

Thus the first want of the spiritual nature, "Who is Jesus?" is met and supplied by the first division of the New Testament—the Gospels. "Many other signs truly did Jesus in the presence of his disciples, which are not written in this book; but these are written that ye might believe that Jesus is the Christ, the Son of God; and believing ye might have life through his name" (John 20: 30, 31). "Believe me that I am in the Father and the Father in me, or else believe me for the very works' sake" (John 14: 11). "Rabbi, we believe thou art a teacher come from God; for no man can do these miracles that thou doest except God be with him" (John 3: 2).

Some years ago this writer made this same argument to one who had recently lost twin children—Willie and Lillie—and had buried them together in the same grave, and had placed at the head of the little mound a twin monument in marble bearing the names of his lost jewels. This father was very near and dear to me by ties of kindred, and I was exceedingly anxious to win him to the Christ. When the argument was finished, I asked him what he thought of it. He answered, "I hardly know what to think of it." I urged him to give a definite answer; for he had listened to it carefully, and was capable of rendering an intelligent decision; but he would not, still claiming that his mind was not quite clear on the subject. I then asked him to imagine a man claiming the power to raise the dead, a power which is found only in God, standing by the grave of his little children. This man has advertised that he is going to call these children back to life; and you and your wife, and a large company of your neighbors, are standing near him, watching and waiting to see the result. The strange man lifts his eyes reverently toward God, and thanks him that he has always heard him, and then he pleads for the sake of those about him that he will hear him once more. After a pause, when a solemn hush, like the silence of the tomb, has settled down over all, the stranger, looking toward the grave where the bodies of the little twins were resting, cries in a clear, strong voice, "Willie and Lillie, come forth!" Instantly the grave opens and your children do come forth, Willie twining his little arms about your neck, and Lillie clasping hers about the neck of her mother. "Under these circumstances," I asked, "what would you think of this strange and wonderful man?" And again he answered that he did not know. But I am sure that he did know; and that he would have fallen at his feet and worshiped him as a divine being.

It is popular in some circles to ignore the miracles altogether; to throw them out of court, as unworthy of consideration by this cultured age. But, before agreeing to this wholesale slaughter of Bible evidence, let it be remembered that the people among whom they were wrought did not deny them. They attempted to discount them by ascribing them to Beelzebub (Mark 3:22); but it was a later age— much later—that discarded them altogether. Suppose a young man, after much research and profound thought (?), decides that the battle of Gettysburg is a myth; no such conflict ever occurred. But when he closes his eloquent address, an old, battle-scarred veteran of Pickett's division, who lost an arm in that famous charge, says: "Young man, that was a fine speech, but it is false; there was such a battle, for it was there I lost my good right arm." Whom shall we believe? The man who was on the ground when the battle was fought, or the man who was born forty years later?

Let it also be remembered that the greatest miracle of all would be that He who is the chief of all miracles should have wrought no miracles. "You may as well expect the sun to send forth darkness as to expect ordinary works from such an extraordinary being."

But more important still, let it never be forgotten that when we give up miracles we give up Christianity.  If there be no miracles, then there was no incarnation, no resurrection, and no ascension, and without these there is no Christianity.

**2. Second Want**  Knowing himself a sinner, and having found the Saviour, the second spiritual want voices itself in the question, "What must I do to be saved?  Here is salvation, how can I appropriate it?"  His teacher turns him to the Book of Acts, the second division of the New Testament.  Here he finds perhaps a half-million people with this same want in their hearts and this same question on their lips; and he finds that all of them heard the gospel, believed it, repented of their sins and were baptized in the name of the Father, Son and Holy Spirit.

This second division of the New Testament, like all the divisions of this Book, is rich and varied in its teachings; but clearly its chief purpose is to show the man in sin how to be saved.  That this is its main purpose is evident in the fact that most of the space is devoted to this subject.  "The greater part of the book," says Prof. J. W. McGarvey, "consists in detailed accounts of conversions to Christ, and of unsuccessful attempts at the same."  After sketching the many accounts of conversions, and attempted conversions, this distinguished Bible teacher, the most eminent in the world on the Book of Acts, says: "Undoubtedly, then, the writer's chief design was to set forth to his readers a multitude of cases of conversion under the labors of the apostles and apostolic men, so that we may know how this work, the main work for which Jesus died, and the apostles were commissioned, was accomplished. The cases recorded represent all the different grades of human society, from idolatrous peasants up to priests, pro-consuls and kings. They represent all the degrees of intellectual and religious culture; all the common occupations of life; and all the countries and lan-guages of the then known world, thus showing the adaptation of the one system of life and salvation to all the inhabitants of the earth."

Those who are away from God and living in sin may be classified as unbelievers, believers, penitent believers and backsliders; and each of these classes has an example or examples illustrative of his con-dition in the Book of Acts, and showing him how to be saved from his sin.

*a.* THE UNBELIEVER. The case of the Philip-pian jailer (16: 16-34) illustrates the unbeliever. He was in the darkness of heathenism, and had to be taught the whole of the plan of salvation: faith to change the heart; repentance to change the life and baptism to change the state or relationship. Faith and baptism are both declared, and repentance is clearly implied, in the washing of the stripes of Paul and Silas.

*b.* THE BELIEVER. The story of Pentecost (2: 1-40) illustrates the man who has faith in Christ, but has not obeyed him. These people are not told to believe, but to repent and be baptized, which would complete their obedience, and deliver them from sin.

*c.* THE PENITENT BELIEVER. The case of Saul

of Tarsus (9: 1-18 and 22: 1-16) illustrates the story of one who has both believed and repented, and hence his obedience is completed by his baptism.

*d.* THE BACKSLIDER. The case of Simon (8: 1-24) illustrates the condition of those who obey the Lord, but afterwards turn from him and go back into sin. He is not told to believe or be baptized, but to repent and pray to God for forgiveness.

Thus is precept illuminated by example, the most effective way of teaching, and also the most successful manner of moving men to action.

Supposing the young Hindoo to have grasped the truth and obeyed it, he is now a Christian and the

**3. Third Want** Of his spiritual nature asserts itself. Gratitude for mercies received, a consuming desire to tell others of his Saviour, and an intense yearning to know more of him, and to become more like him, is the great purpose of his life. The song of his heart is:

> "More about Jesus would I know,
> More of his grace to others show;
> More of his saving fullness see,
> More of his love who died for me.

> "More about Jesus let me learn,
> More of his holy will discern;
> Spirit of God, my teacher be,
> Showing the things of Christ to me.

> "More about Jesus, in his word,
> Holding communion with my Lord;
> Hearing his voice in every line,
> Making each faithful saying mine."

His teacher now directs him in the study of the Epistles, the third division of the New Testament. Beginning with Romans, each of these twenty-one books is studied, and they are found to be directed to Christians to show them how to live the Christian life. He hears Paul talking to a young man like himself, and saying, "Study to show thyself approved unto God, a workman that needeth not to be ashamed, rightly dividing the word of truth" (2 Tim. 2:15). Again he hears this father in the gospel exhorting his son in these words: "These things I write unto thee, hoping to come unto thee shortly; but if I tarry long, that thou mayest know how thou oughtest to behave thyself in the house of God, which is the church of the living God, the pillar and ground of the truth" (1 Tim. 3:14, 15). He also reads from the Roman letter (1:1, 2): "I beseech you, therefore, brethren, by the mercies of God, that ye present your bodies a living sacrifice, holy, acceptable unto God, which is your reasonable service." And from 1 Cor. 3:9, he reads: "For we are laborers together with God; ye are God's husbandry, ye are God's building."

His soul revels in the richness of these and kindred Scriptures, and he is soon active and useful in the church. Wherever duty calls he responds, and whenever the door of opportunity opens he enters in. He grows in grace and in the knowledge of the Lord Jesus Christ, and becomes a pillar in the temple of God.

The Christian of to-day ought to learn anew this old lesson, for we are saved to serve. In spiritual things as in natural, the inexorable law of life is *do* or *die*. The unused arm withers, the unused eye loses the power of vision, and the idle brain loses the power of thought. The Jordan waters, as they come down from the snow-covered mountains of Lebanon, are clear as crystals, beautiful as diamonds, and full of life. But when they enter the fatal sea and become inactive, they die.

The Master's life, the model for the lives of his disciples, was one of service. At the early age of twelve he said: "I must be about my Father's business" (Luke 2:49). In the midst of his ministry, he said: "I must work the work of him that sent me while it is day; the night cometh, when no man can work" (John 9:4). When Peter would sum up in a single short sentence the key to His wonderful life, he says, "He went about doing good" (Acts 10:38). There will be but two classes at the judgment: those who did and those who did not (Matt. 25:31-46).

The supreme want of the church is workers: active, tireless, consecrated and strong, who can be relied upon; men and women not only built on the rock, but of the rock: granite Christians (1 Pet. 2:5). The task committed to her hands is nothing less than the salvation of a lost world: a gigantic undertaking. To bring it thus far has cost the blood of an army of martyrs, and the sacrifice of the Lord Jesus Christ. May we pray and labor for power sufficient for this great task.

A little child was asked why she wished to be a painter. "That I may help God paint the skies and

clouds at sunset," was the reply. But God wants
no such help. In arching the skies, in piling up
mountains, in painting the rainbow, and in the thousands of other works, he has no human partner. He
asks not our help in burnishing the sun, in keeping
the moon and stars in their orbits, or in beautifying
and sweetening the roses, and in making gorgeous
the garments of the birds. But in the greatest of
all work, the saving of souls, he honors us by making
us his coworkers.

Now let us at a single bound pass over a half
century of time, and find ourselves in the house of
this same man, now fourscore years of age. The
eyes once so clear and bright are now dim; the ears
once so sensitive to sound are now dull; the hair
once black as the raven's wing is now white as
snow; and the manly form once erect and strong
now stoops and staggers under the weight of years.
He is no longer able to meet with his brethren in
public worship; his active work has all been turned
over to others; and, sitting there on the summit of
a long and fruitful life, he gazes yearningly into the
future. He has been so busy hitherto that he has
had little time for thoughts of this kind. His old
teacher is still at his elbow, and he recognizes in all
this the

**4. Fourth Want** Of his spiritual nature; and he
opens the Book of Revlation, the
fourth division of the New Testament, the pro-
phetic department, that this want may be supplied.
He reads to him: "Blessed are the dead who die in
the Lord from henceforth; yea, saith the Spirit, that

they may rest from their labors; and their works do follow them" (14:13). The old man puts his hand to his ear, saying, "My hearing is not as keen as it once was; please repeat that verse to me;" and it is repeated slowly and distinctly. "Thank God for that precious passage," he continued. "It pronounces a blessing on those who die 'in the Lord.' I have been in him for fifty years and I am soon to die. And it promises 'rest.' I am tired. The long, rough road has worn me out. And now as a tender mother at the close of day rocks the tired child to sleep, so God will lay my wearied body down to rest in the bosom of the earth till the resurrection morn. But this is not all. It says my works are to follow me. I have not done much, it is true, but I have done something; and these little waves of influence which I placed in motion, like pebbles dropped in the sea, will continue to roll on long after I am gone, and they will never stop until they reach the shores of eternity."

His teacher quotes another passage: "And God shall wipe away all tears from their eyes; and there shall be no more death, neither sorrow nor crying; neither shall there be any more pain, for the former things are passed away" (21:4). His old face brightens, and he praises God that there will be no pain, no sorrow, no tears and no death in the home to which he is going.

A third time his reader quotes to him: "Blessed are they who do his commandments, that they may have right to the tree of life, and may enter in through the gates into the city" (22:14). Again this ripe old saint breaks forth in praise. "I remember," he says, "that in Eden, before sin came, our parents held sweet communion with God, and dwelt near the tree of life. But when sin entered they were driven out into the cold, dark world; but in Christ we are to regain all this, and to retain it forever and forever." And with this last utterance the angels came and bore his yearning spirit back to God.

A wonderful book is this. It found this young man groping his way in darkness, and it gave him light. It first led him to the Christ, the Son of God, and the Saviour of men. It next told him how to be saved. It then led him in ways of usefulness and joy as a Christian. And finally it opened the grave for him and hung a light in its dark vault; it unbolted the gates of the New Jerusalem and ushered him into the presence of the tree of life, and God wiped all his tears away. How shall we account for its perfect adaptation to the wants of man? There is but one way: each has a common author. The Being who created man with these fourfold wants is the Author of this book with its fourfold supplies.

## REVIEW.

1. Why is the New Testament of special interest to us?

2. Is it systematically arranged?

3. Give the first want and first division.

4. What four miracles were studied by the Hindoo?

5. What was the purpose of the miracles?

6. Give the incident of "Willie and Lillie."

7. What is the second want and second division?

8. Give the four classes outside the church.

9. Give the third want and third division.

10. Give the fourth want and fourth division.

11. What three passages are studied by the Hindoo?

# IV.

# THE WISDOM AND PURITY OF THE CHRIST

# OUTLINE—CHAPTER IV.

1. MANIFESTATIONS OF WISDOM.
   a. THE WISDOM OF CHILDHOOD.
   b. THE SERMON ON THE MOUNT.
   c. CHURCH AND STATE.
   d. MARRIAGE IN HEAVEN.
   e. THE GREAT COMMANDMENT.
   f. THE ADULTEROUS WOMAN.
   g. THE PARABLES.

2. PECULIARITIES.
   a. HE MADE NO MISTAKES.
   b. HE SPOKE WITHOUT EFFORT.
   c. HE SPOKE WITHOUT HESITATION OR CONSULTATION.
   d. HE NEVER EXPRESSED A DOUBT.
   e. HIS LANGUAGE SUPREMELY SIMPLE.
   f. HE COMBINED MARVELOUS SWEEP, PERFECTION AND POWER.
   g. HIS WORDS ARE FULL OF INSPIRATION.
   h. HIS TEACHINGS ARE SMALL IN BULK.

3. HOW ACCOUNT FOR ALL THIS.
   a. NOT BY LONG LIFE AND EXPERIENCE.
   b. NOT BY SUPERIOR ADVANTAGES.
   c. BUT BECAUSE HE IS GOD MANIFEST IN THE FLESH.

4. MANIFESTATIONS OF PURITY.
   a. FREEDOM FROM SELFISHNESS.
   b. FREEDOM FROM AMBITION.

# IV.

## THE WISDOM AND PURITY OF THE CHRIST.

In our studies thus far we have settled, we hope, three important points: the existence of God, the Bible as his message to man, and the perfect adaptation of the New Testament to our spiritual wants. In the last of these studies we found the Christ, and saw something of his wonderful power—sufficient, perhaps, for our present purposes. But in this and in our next two studies we will linger about him. He is so inseparably associated with Christianity that he must have a large place in the study of its first principles. We can not ignore the sun while we study astronomy.

Our present purpose is to show that his wisdom and purity prove his divinity. "Never man spake like this man" (John 7:46). If he is divine, this must be true. His speech must not be that of man with his faults and frailties, but the voice of God, and perfect as its Author.

**1. Manifestations of His Wisdom** *a.* THE WISDOM OF CHILD-HOOD. Doubtless His mother, when we see her, will tell us that while he was a little boy playing about her knees, he said many strangely wise things for one of his years. But so far as the records show, his wisdom was first manifested in his twelfth year. His parents had taken him to Jerusalem. What wonders

greeted his vision. The great buildings, the mag-
nificent court, the impressive ritualism, the solemn
sacrifices, the sublime music, and the millions of
worshipers, must have deeply impressed his young
mind. But these were not the most impressive
things. The temple was the seat of Jewish knowledge. There their teachers met in council; there
their Scriptures were interpreted; there the law was
expounded; and so interested was the boy in all this
that when his parents started on the homeward
journey he lingered in this delightful atmosphere.
A search was made for him, and he was found in
the midst of these teachers, hearing them and asking
them questions (Luke 2:46). How we wish we
knew some of the questions he asked. But we will
have to wait till we pass over to the other side.

*b.* THE SERMON ON THE MOUNT. Even at the
risk of being called sacrilegious, I venture to say
that this old and revered title "Sermon on the
Mount" is largely a misnomer. This is no mere
sermon, but rather the inaugural address of our
King as he mounts his throne and begins his reign;
a general summary of the principles in the charter
of the new government.

Is it feeble and commonplace? Does it savor of
the spirit and thought of the time and place in
which it was spoken? Does it not rise above these
like the dome of heaven rises above the earth? Is
not every word and sentence as fresh as when they
fell from the gracious lips of the great Teacher?
Does it not contain the germs of individual and
national civilization, and the truth by which a lost

world is to be saved? Does it not bear the unmistakable impress of heaven?

*c.* CHURCH AND STATE. Few questions are more complex than that of church and state. And the Pharisees and Herodians, anxious to involve Christ in their party quarrels, asked him whether it was lawful to pay taxes to Rome. A shrewd trap truly. Whatever the answer, he must be entangled. If he answers "Yes," the Jews will turn against him. If the answer is "No," the Romans will arrest him as a rebel against Cæsar. But his answer is neither "Yes" nor "No." He called for a penny, bearing the image and superscription of the Roman emperor, and said, "Render unto Cæsar the things that are Cæsar's, and unto God the things that are God's," and thus laid down the only principle by which this vexed question can be settled (Matt. 22:15-22).

*d.* MARRIAGE IN HEAVEN. The Sadducee, with his coarse conceptions, incapable of thinking on spiritual things, thought to entangle Him on the subject of marriage in the future world. They tell him of a woman who had seven husbands, and the seven were brothers, and ask, if there is to be such a world, whose wife will she be. He told them that life would be continuous, but that the true life was spiritual, not fleshly, and therefore the future life, as regarding marriage, would be like that of the angels (Matt. 22:23-30).

*e.* THE GREAT COMMANDMENT.. The Talmud says there are 613 commandments—248 positive and 365 negative—and none but an angel could keep them, hence their anxiety to find one comprehensive

enough to embrace them all, and so he is asked:
"Master, which is the great commandment in the
law? Jesus said unto them, Thou shalt love the
Lord thy God with all thy heart, and with all thy
soul, and with all thy mind." Here they would have
had him stop; for in their selfishness and conceit
they recognized no obligation to others. But he
did not stop, but continued: "This is the first and
great commandment; but the second is like unto it,
Thou shalt love thy neighbor as thyself. On these
two commandments hang all the law and the prophets" (Matt. 22: 34-40).

*f.* THE ADULTEROUS WOMAN. And when these
sanctimonious hypocrites, knowing his mercy to the
erring, seek to involve him in a controversy with
Moses, he drove the truth into their guilty consciences by saying, "He that is without sin among
you, let him first cast a stone at her;" and they,
"being convicted by their own conscience, went out
cne by one, beginning at the eldest, even unto the
last." And turning to the woman, he asked: "Where
are those thine accusers? Hath no man condemned
thee? She said, No man, Lord. And Jesus said
unto her, Neither do I condemn thee; go and sin
no more" (John 8: 3-11).

*g.* THE PARABLES. Much of the Master's teaching was parabolic, the simplest, and yet the most difficult method of teaching. At first sight one feels that
any one could use it. But here, as everywhere else,
Christ is inimitable. These parables refuse to be
duplicated. A brainy unbeliever once declared his
ability to duplicate them, and promised to do it in

one day. But at night he asked for more time, and another day was given. When it was gone he still wanted time, and a week was added. Then a month, and then three months, when he gave up the effort, saying he believed them beyond the power of man. And such is the conviction of those who have studied them most. They grow bigger and brighter the more we study them; and what at first seemed a surface truth, deepens into a fathomless sea; and the margins apparently so near together become as wide as the world.

Schaff well says: "Christ's intellect is truly marvelous; he was never deceived by appearances; he penetrated through the surface, and always went straight to the heart and marrow; he never asked a question which was not perfectly appropriate; he never gave an answer which was not fully to the point, or which could be better conceived or exressed, How often did he silence his cavilers, the shrewd and cunning priests and scribes, by a short sentence which hit the nail on the head, or struck like lightning into their conscience, or wisely evaded the trap laid for him. Is such an intellect clear as the sky, bracing as the mountain air, sharp and penetrating as a sword, thoroughly healthy and vigorous, always ready and always self-possessed"—is this the intellect of a mere man? Is he but one in many of the world's great thinkers? Is he not rather the many in one—totalized humanity? Is his not a voice divine?

**2. Peculiarities** There are striking peculiarities about the wisdom of Christ which argue with equal force his divinity.

*a.* HE MADE NO MISTAKES.  Other great teachers, as Socrates, Plato and Aristotle, often confess their errors.  But Christ made no such confession.  And the shrewd enemies who watched his every word and work, failed to find a mistake.

*b.* HE SPOKE WITHOUT EFFORT.  Other famous men often reach dizzy summits, but it is after long and labored effort.  But he speaks the highest truth in simplest tones, and there is no sign of weariness; no more than in the mountain spring from which fresh, sweet water is always gushing.

*c.* HE SPOKE WITHOUT HESITATION OR CONSULTATION.  The wisest men hesitate and consult before venturing an answer on great questions.  But Christ, whatever the question, always answered promptly, and without counsel.  On the green grass, on the bow of the boat, on the mountain-side, in the home, in the synagogue, everywhere this was true.

*d.* HE NEVER EXPRESSED A DOUBT.  Even great Socrates often left his disciples in doubt.  Of immortality he said: "If death is a removal hence to another place, and if what is said of death is true, then those who live in Hades are henceforth immortal."  And among his last words, after receiving the fatal cup, he said: "The hour of separation has come; I go to die, and you to live; but as to which of us is destined to an improved being is concealed from every one except God."  But however intricate and difficult the theme, Christ always spoke with absolute assurance.

*e.* HIS LANGUAGE WAS SUPREMELY SIMPLE. Goldsmith says of Johnson: "You make your little

fish talk like whales." And many others have this
fondness for swollen language. But Christ spoke of
the loftiest subjects in the simplest language. Who
ever needs a dictionary to study his words? His language is simple enough for a primer, and yet each
word sparkles like a gem, and his sentences and sermons dazzle like a cabinet filled with diamonds. No
wonder the common people heard him gladly.

*f.* HE COMBINED MARVELOUS SWEEP, PERFECTION
AND POWER. Read the parable of the prodigal son.
Note its mastery of principles; its breadth of vision;
its knowledge of the human heart; its simplicity of
definition and its grasping and grouping of details.
One might as well attempt to brighten the sun or
sweeten the rose as to try to improve this masterpiece
in composition. And Dickens, supreme in the
pathetic style, when asked for the most pathetic
story in literature, answered, "The Prodigal Son."

*g.* HIS WORDS ARE FULL OF INSPIRATION.
Shakespeare has inspired many during the three hundred years since he wrote. It is claimed that "twelve
great students of four nationalities" have written
commentaries on his dramas. This is remarkable.
But no admirer of the bard of Stratford has been
inspired by him to leave home and loved ones and
go to darkest Africa to give the message of his
adored master to the people there. Yet during the
last century alone the intellectual stimulus of
Christ's words has been so great that more than
two hundred dictionaries and grammars, in as many
different languages and dialects, have been given
to the world.

*h.* HIS TEACHINGS ARE SMALL IN BULK. We regret that no shorthand reporter was there to catch every word of wisdom as it fell from his lips, and so we have but little of his teaching. Augustine uses thirty volumes to systematize his theology; and Calvin uses forty; and Paul writes more of the New Testament than does its Lord. We can easily read all he said in a single hour. He seemed not to care to preserve his words, but cast them abroad like the sower does the seed, knowing that they would not return unto him void, but would accomplish that whereunto they were sent (Isa. 55: 11).

**3. How Account for All This**        There must be a solution for this strange problem. What is it?

*a.* IT IS NOT HIS LONG LIFE AND RICH EXPERIENCE. Socrates was threescore and ten when he drank the fatal poison; and Plato was eleven years older when he died. But Christ was only thirty-three when they nailed him to the cross.

*b.* IT IS NOT HIS SUPERIOR ADVANTAGES. The world's famous teachers have generally been life-long students under the most favorable circumstances. Plato, Aristotle, Zeno, etc., spent their lives in studying books and listening to living teachers. And they traversed the world in search of knowledge. They sat at the feet of the priests, sages and philosophers of Egypt, India, Italy and Greece. But Christ had no schools except the very poor ones of his people, and no books except the Old Testament, and he was too busy at the carpenter's bench to go to the world's famous teachers, and there were no great ones in Galilee.

*c.* BECAUSE HE IS GOD MANIFEST IN THE FLESH. In the eloquent language of another we close: "Without science and learning he has shed more light on things human and divine than all other scholars and philosophers combined. Without the eloquence of the schools he has spoken such words of beauty and power as were never spoken before or since. Without writing a single line, he has set in motion more pens, furnished themes for more sermons, orations, discussions, and sublime poems and works of art, than whole armies of great men of ancient and modern times. He has built a pyramid of knowledge to which no man has made an addition in two thousand years."

**4. Manifestations of His Purity** If Jesus is divine, he must be as perfect in purity as we have found him in wisdom; and if he is thus perfect, he is divine. Here the issue is sharply drawn, for what greater exception in human life than to find a sinless man?

Plutarch says: "The evil passions of men are inborn, and not introduced from without; and if strict discipline did not come to the aid, man would hardly be tamer than the wildest beast." Seneca says: "All is full of crime and vice. Iniquity prevails in every heart; and innocence has not only become rare, but has entirely disappeared." And Marcus Aurelius says: "Faithfulness, sense of honor, righteousness and truth have taken their flight from the wide earth to heaven."

And this testimony from heathendom is corroborated by the church. The entire Christian world, Greek, Latin and Protestant, is a unit as to the universality of sin. Even the Virgin Mary is not an exception, for her sinlessness is explained in a Papal decision of 1854, as the result of a miraculous interposition, and the reflex influence of her holy Son.

But, bad as was the world at large, there was never a worse age and place than those of the advent of Christ. When he looked out from the manger of Bethlehem he saw a world rotten to the core. This was specially true of Palestine, and in Palestine there was no spot quite so bad as Nazareth. It was so corrupt that there was a proverb: "No good thing cometh out of Nazareth." It was the headquarters of the Roman legions, and, maelstrom-like, had sucked into its voracious maw all evil. There is no such place of corruption as a mass of men with no women except those who are bad. The best people fled from the place as from a pestilence. And yet it was here Christ spent his childhood, youth and manhood, and it was here he grew into the fairest flower that ever bloomed in the gardens of God. Like the water-lily in the filthy slough, he developed the whiteness and purity of the snow despite his surroundings.

This is the high claim we make for our Christ. We assert that he is the only one who has carried the spotless purity of childhood through youth and manhood; the only one who has passed through life, touching it at every point, and then emerging from the tomb and going back to the bosom of the Father as pure as when he came. And this is the claim he makes for himself. Speaking to those who were thirsting for his blood, he said: "Who of you convicteth me of sin?" (John 8:46). And this challenge has been ringing down through the ages from that day to this, and no man has yet been able to convict him of sin.

In the light of the law of environment this is marvelous. Man has been called a creature of circumstances. He seldom rises above his surroundings, and his early influences usually cling to him through life, making or marring his character. No one expects the powers of resistance in the hothouse plant, and no one expects them absent from the storm-shaken oak on the unsheltered hills. Oliver Twist never fully recovered from his stay in Fagin's den, and Jean Valjean never cast off the influence of his convict life. But Christ, the Sun of righteousness (Mal. 4:2), was as little contaminated by the evils which surrounded him as is the king of day who lights and purifies the filthy earth.

Let us now note this thought in detail:

*a.* HE WAS FREE FROM SELFISHNESS. This detestable vice, so abhorred in others, and yet so common in ourselves, had no place in him. It was he who said: "It is more blessed to give than to receive." And when we imbibe this spirit we move out from the lowlands of selfishness, where every drop of blood is poisoned, and we are sick and barren, to the highlands of benevolence, where is perpetual health, joy and fruitfulness. Renan says: "He is free from all selfishness, the source of our sorrow, and thought only of his work, his race and humanity."

*b*. HE WAS FREE FROM AMBITION. He was ambitious, it is true, but it was a holy ambition. He would reign, but only in the hearts of men; and for them he freely gave his love, his life, and his heart's blood. His ambition was unlike that of Cyrus, Alexander and Napoleon as vice is unlike virtue, as right is unlike wrong. His people once pressed him to take a crown, but he departed from them into a mountain that he might be alone with his Father (John 6: 15). *"Ecce Homo"* says: "We scarcely know which to admire most, the prodigious originality of his conceptions, or his entire freedom from worldly ambition in the execution of his plans."

*c*. HE WAS FREE FROM PRIDE. This was the first sin to enter the human heart, and it seems determined to be the last to leave it. Give man money, position and power, and he is filled with pride. When the flowers are fullest of the dews of heaven, and when the wheat is richest and ripest, they bow their heads in gratitude; but the more we are enriched of God, the higher our heads. But how different the Christ. When he preached his great sermons he acted as if there were scores about him who could have done better. After his stupendous miracles he seemed unconscious of the fact that he was the only being on earth who could do such deeds. When he lifted the heavy heel of death from the heart of Lazarus he walked away from the grave as if he were leaving the carpenter's shop after a day of ordinary toil.

*d.* HE WAS FREE FROM COVETOUSNESS. This sin is well-nigh universal among men, but there is no trace of it in the Saviour. He might have had millions for his cures, and yet he lived and died the poorest of the poor. "The foxes have holes, and the birds of the air have nests, but the Son of man hath not where to rest his head" (Matt. 8: 20). He was so poor that a miracle was necessary to pay his temple tax (Matt. 17: 24-27). And he was so poor in death that his body rested in a borrowed grave (Matt. 27: 59, 60).

*e.* HE WAS FREE FROM REVENGE. Plato, being told that some one was circulating slanderous and malicious reports about him, said: "What of it? I will take care to so live that none will believe them." How beautiful the thought that a pure life is its own best defense; and how noble the heart that would only silence, not harm, an enemy. But Christ seeks not simply to silence, but to save, his foes. When in the death agony of Calvary, he prayed: "Father, forgive them; they know not what they do." And when he sent his disciples forth to save men, he told them to go first to Jerusalem and preach to those who murdered him.

*f.* HE WAS FREE FROM SECTARIANISM. How great the difference between Jesus and the great men of the world at this point. They are sectional, but he is universal. They are identified with some particular people and age, and partake of their peculiarities.  Even great Moses, who is honored and revered in three religions, is not only a Jew by birth, but he is also a Jew in feelings, habit and thought.  Demosthenes rose high in his day, but he never rose above the Greek type of thought and character.  Luther can never be understood if not studied as a German.  Calvin, though exiled from his native land, lived and died a Frenchman.  And our beloved Washington can never be to another people what he is to Americans.  The vision and influence of these choice spirits extend far beyond their nation and time, but they are not universal. But what they were to their particular people, place and age, Christ is to all.  And this despite the dominant idea of his people.  They thought he was to be a king, but it was to be emphatically a Jewish king; he was to reign over the world, but his throne, with its special privileges, was to be in Jerusalem.  Every teacher, including his father and mother, endeavored to impress him with this thought.  Yet this young Hebrew carpenter so conquered the sectarianism about him that he rose above the walls of separation between Jew and Gentile as completely as if he had lived on another planet.  He is the one universal character, the one sole cosmopolitan.  He was the ideal Jew, or they would not have tried to force their crown upon him; he is equally the ideal of the polished Greeks, who, when they see him in his beauty, forget their hatred of the Jew in their admiration of him.  And the same is true when he is preached to the war-like Roman, the liberty-loving German, the dark-

6

browed African, the clannish Chinaman, the pro-
gressive Japanese, the cultured. Englishman, the
elegant Frenchman, the sturdy Scotchman and the
wide-awake American. Each sees in him his ideal.
Like the sun, he can not be monopolized by any,
but shines equally for all.

**5. Completeness of His Character** The virtues just enumerated
are not all that are found in the
character of Jesus. They are only
specimens. All are there. Not a
single gem is absent from the tiara of moral beauty
which encircles his brow. And they are not only
present, but they are perfectly blended. Nothing
is out of proportion; the symmetry is complete.
There is no one-sidedness in him. No one virtue
towered above the rest, but each was moderated
and completed by its opposite grace. His character
never lost its equilibrium, and hence never needed
readjustment or modification. He was vivacious
without levity; vigorous without violence; serious
without melancholy; dignified without pride or pre-
sumption. He combined the strength of the lion
with the meekness of the lamb, and the wisdom
of the serpent with the harmlessness of the dove.
Every element of character finds in him the hap-
piest harmony—harmony like that in the summer
and winter, and in the day and night.

Let the reader remember that this is wisdom
and purity combined. The brainiest men are not
always the best; and their friends frequently have
to insist that their lack of moral worth should be
atoned for by mental fiber. We are to see the

genius as he soars in the heavens rather than **the** sinner as he walks on the earth. Byron could dwell among the stars, while his heart fed on carrion. Burns could sing like an angel, but, alas! he did not live like one. And Burr was brilliant but bad. Not so with the Christ. His heart is as pure as his head is clear. His life is without blot or blemish, and has neither parallel nor approach. And herein, perhaps more than at any other single point, is the seat of his power over men. In the French Revolution, when the mob, wild with rage, swept like a flood through the streets of Paris, destroying everything in its way, a well-known man, of pure and noble character, came into its presence and waved his hand for a hearing. The leader commanded a halt, and said, "Soldiers, we are in the presence of a man who represents seventy years of noble living;" and the mob uncovered its head and listened. It was a great thing to say of Jesus, "Never man spake like this man;" but it is greater to say, "Never man lived like this man."

**6. A Few Witnesses** We close by calling a few of the myriads of witnesses who have testified for him. Some are friends and some are foes, but as to his purity there is but one voice. Pilate's wife, with the seldom erring instinct of woman, warned her husband in these words: "Have thou nothing to do with that just man." And when Pilate, weak and wavering, delivered him up to be crucified, he washed his hands in the presence of the mob he feared, and said: "I am innocent of the blood of this just person." Judas, the betrayer, brought back the thirty pieces of silver and cast them at the feet of those who gave it, saying: "I have sinned in that I have betrayed innocent blood." The centurion and soldiers who executed him said: "Truly this was the Son of God."

Besides these who saw him in the flesh, let us hear others of a later day. Rousseau: "If the life and death of Socrates are those of a sage, the life and death of Jesus are those of a God." Napoleon: "I know men; and I tell you that Jesus Christ is not a man." Channing: "Jesus not only was, he is still, the Son of God, the Saviour of the world." Strauss: "Christ represents within the religious sphere the highest point, beyond which posterity can never go." Jean Paul: "Jesus is the purest among the mighty, and the mightiest among the pure." Renan: "Whatever may be the surprises of the future, Jesus will never be surpassed. Repose now in thy glory, thy work is finished, thy divinity is established. A thousand times more living, a thousand times more loved since thy death, than during the days of thy course here below, thou shalt become the corner-stone of humanity, insomuch that to tear thy name from the world would be to shake it to its very foundations. No more shall men distinguish between thee and God."

## REVIEW.

1. Name the seven proofs of superior wisdom.
2. Give Schaff's comment.

3. Mention eight peculiarities of Christ's wisdom.

4. How account for this wonderful wisdom?

5. What of the law of environment as applied to the Christ?

6. Name six examples of Christ's purity.

7. What of the "completeness" of the Christ life?

8. Name nine witnesses on the question of Christ's divinity.

# V
# THE RESURRECTION OF CHRIST

# OUTLINE—CHAPTER V.

1. CONCEDED FACTS.
2. INFIDEL POSITION.
3. CHRISTIAN POSITION.
4. THE TRILEMMA.
    *a.* WERE THEY DECEIVED?
    *b.* WERE THEY DECEIVERS?
    *c.* THEY WERE RELIABLE WITNESSES.
5. CORROBORATIVE TESTIMONY.
    *a.* INFLUENCE OF THE RESURRECTION ON THE DISCIPLES.
    *b.* TRIUMPH OF THE TRUTH.
    *c.* THE LORD'S SUPPER.
    *d.* THE LORD'S DAY.

# V.

## THE RESURRECTION OF CHRIST.

Having seen the power of God manifested in the miracles of Christ, the knowledge of God in his wisdom, and the purity of God in his life, we might rest the claims of his divinity; but we wish to make certainty doubly sure by witnessing the climax of proof in his resurrection from the dead. Paul names the resurrection (Heb. 6:1, 2) as one of the things belonging to the principles of the doctrine of Christ, and he hinges everything on it. "If Christ be not raised, your faith is vain; ye are yet in your sins" (1 Cor. 15:17). This is the key to the whole question. If this greatest of all miracles is true, then there need be no question about the supernatural; but, if false, we might as well end the whole matter now and here and give up all hope. If he rose from the dead, Christianity is true; if not, it is false.

**1. Conceded Facts** There are some important facts conceded by all, which should be noted in the beginning of this investigation. It is conceded that Jesus of Nazareth lived at the time and place ascribed to him in the New Testament; that he was crucified in Jerusalem during the reign of Pontius Pilate; that his body was buried in Joseph's new tomb; that a great stone was laid at the mouth of the tomb, and that on the morning of the third day the body was gone.

**2. The Infidel Position**
On Sunday morning, when it was discovered that the body was gone, the soldiers came into the city and reported the fact to the chief priests, and they called a council and gave large money to the soldiers, saying: "Say ye, His disciples came by night, and stole him away while we slept. And if this come to the governor's ears, we will persuade him, and save you. So they took the money, and did as they were taught" (Matt. 28: 11-15).

In support of this position they could command the testimony of sixty witnesses, an ample number, who were on the ground—the right place—for the purpose of guarding the tomb.

But before we hear them, let us remember that three of the strongest motives ever used by Satan for the corruption of a witness were used in this case: disgrace, bribery and death. Every soldier would shrink from the disgrace of having a body committed to his care stolen; money has made its millions swerve from the right; and all men in their normal condition love life, and a Roman guard forfeited his own when he allowed his prisoner to escape.

Let us hear these witnesses. Behold sixty bronzed veterans filing into the witness-box and each saying that the body was stolen while they were guarding the tomb. This is an unreasonable story. If they had said a large force had overpowered them and taken the body from them, it would, other things being equal, have been reasonable. But it is not thinkable that sixty veteran soldiers, familiar with guard duty, in charge of a safe filled with valuables, would not only sleep—all of them at the same time—but would sleep so soundly that thieves could rifle the safe and escape with the treasure without waking one of them. This is unbelievable.

But, bad as this is, it is not the worst. Ask these gentlemen what they were doing at the time of the theft, and they say they were sleeping. This adds absurdity to unreasonableness. If they were asleep, how did they know that the body was stolen? And, if stolen, how did they know that the disciples stole it? Their story is false on its face; and such witnesses would be ruled out of any court of justice.

But the tissue of absurdities connected with their story is not yet complete. If the body was stolen, why did they not require the timid disciples to bring it back? One public exhibition of that mangled form—so well known—would have settled at one fell blow, and for all time, the story of Jesus and the resurrection.

3. The Christian Position

The witnesses in this case are more than five hundred, and they saw him frequently during a period of forty days after the resurrection, and talked and ate with him. The number is ample, as in the other case, and their means of knowledge all that could be desired. And in addition to this, and of the most vital importance, remember that there were no motives for them to testify falsely. But, on the other hand, everything which is hard to bear, and which men instinctively try to avoid— shame, persecution and death—stood out luridly before them as their inevitable fate.

**4. The Trilemma**        The truth must be somewhere in this trilemma: they were de- ceived, they were deceivers, or they were reliable witnesses.

*a.* WERE THEY DECEIVED? Their mental condi- tion forbade deception. Every one of them, inclu- ding those keen-visioned women, expected an earthly kingdom. That was why the mother of James and John requested the chief places for her sons; that was why Peter and others, thinking all was lost, returned to their fishing-boats; that was why the two disciples, on their way to Emmaus, were so sad and hopeless. And up to the time of his ascen- sion this thought clung to them: "Lord, wilt thou at this time restore the kingdom to Israel?" (Acts 1:6). The resurrection of Jesus was as far from their thoughts as his visible appearance is from the thought of the reader of these lines at this time.

They saw him too often to be deceived. I have been preaching in this city for twenty-four years; have associated with the people in the church, on the streets, and in their homes; have been with them in their glad days and their sad ones—at the mar- riage altar, and by the open grave—and they know me. Suppose I should disappear, and be gone for three days; after which, for a period of forty days, I should meet and mingle with five hundred of them, talking and eating with them, would they know me? This is the parallel as to Christ, and it must carry conviction to the heart of every unbiased reader.

"But did they not doubt?" (Matt. 28:17). Yes, some of them did doubt. But what of it? That fact makes them the more reliable as witnesses. It shows that they were not the credulous dupes some would have us believe them to be, but honest searchers after truth, ready and determined to sift all the facts regarding the resurrection. And let it never be forgotten that after this examination their doubts vanished. Thomas, the chief doubter, after the fullest possible examination of the case, cried, "My Lord and my God!" (John 20:28). And of the others, after a similar investigation, it was said: "And none of the disciples durst ask him, Who art thou? knowing that it was the Lord" (John 21:1-12).

*b.* WERE THEY DECEIVERS? There was no motive for deception, and sane men like these always act from motive. No one had offered them money as they did the soldiers; and there was no popularity to gain, for it now looked like a lost cause. On the other hand, they had all to lose. But, in spite of this, if he did not rise, they told a deliberate falsehood, and one diametrically opposed to their every interest, both for time and for eternity. Would you do such a thing as this? They gave the highest possible evidence of their honesty. As soon as they began to preach the resurrection their persecutions began. They were thrust into prison, but released with the command to desist from their preaching. Then they were scourged. Soon Stephen became the first martyr, and with his dying breath he declared that he saw the risen Christ standing on the right hand of God. Next James was beheaded, and Peter was waiting for the day of execution. And thus it continued until nearly all of them were slain; but not one of them changed his testimony; not a single one of them turned "state's evidence."

c. THEY WERE RELIABLE WITNESSES. The truth must be in this third horn of the trilemma, for there is no other reasonable explanation of their conduct.

Greenleaf, perhaps the highest authority on evidence that ever lived, has thoroughly sifted this evidence, and here is his conclusion: "Let the witnesses be compared with themselves, with each other, and with surrounding facts and circumstances; and let their testimony be sifted as if it were given in a court of justice on the side of the adverse party, the witnesses being subjected to a vigorous cross-examination. The result, it is confidently believed, will be an undoubting conviction of their integrity, ability and truth. In the course of such an examination the undesigned coincidences will multiply upon us at every step in our progress; the probability of the veracity of the witnesses and of the reality of the occurrences which they relate will increase until it acquires, for all practical purposes, the value and force of demonstration."

Let us glance at some

**5. Corroborative Testimony**

*a.* THE INFLUENCE OF THE RESURRECTION ON THE DISCIPLES. It must be sadly confessed that before the resurrection his disciples were anything but ideal followers of their Master. They were slow to learn, and selfish; and in his hour of sore need one betrayed him and others forsook him and fled. And when he was crucified what would one naturally expect of them? Would we not expect them, crushed in spirit and disappointed in hope, to disperse and sink into oblivion, "leaving only the record of another prophet's failure to be reckoned with that of Theudas, and Judas of Galilee, and similar sporadic flashes of Jewish fanaticism"? But we find nothing of the kind. Those arrant cowards became bold as lions, defying both the religious venom of the Jew and the political rage of the Roman. Their soul-vision is unclouded, and their voices ring out, clear-toned like trumpets, as they proclaim the sweet story of their risen Lord. All this must be accounted for. Every effect has a cause, and this effect could "no more have risen out of nothing, or come about by chance, than our great modern railroad system could have arisen spontaneously in a land where iron was unknown, or have been developed without the brain of a Watt and the genius of a Stephenson."

*b.* THE TRIUMPH OF THE TRUTH IN THE FACE OF OPPOSITION. Ballard forcefully says: "If we can imagine a lion, a tiger and a wolf uniting in desperate effort to destroy a lamb—and failing—we should but have a fair parallel to that which actually happened in human society at the commencement of the Christian era. The practical alliance betwen Jewish hate, Roman might and Greek subtlety, against the infant Christian faith, is absolutely without parallel in history." But in the face of this mighty alliance, the new doctrine spread with wonderful rapidity. The first sermon gained three thousand converts; a second sermon, five thousand; and soon these converts were no longer counted, but referred to as multitudes, so that in the brief record of the Book of Acts not less than half a million Christians are made. And within twenty-five years after the crucifixion the unhesitating belief in the resurrection was established among all Christians throughout the then known world.

Many of these converts were from the Jews, including priests, and other great men like Saul of Tarsus. And if the reader thinks men of this kind are easily converted, let him try to induce some modern rabbi to accept the Christ.

And as to the persecutions encountered in this work, neither the language of men nor angels can do justice to their horror, or to the heroism of those who endured them. But a single quotation from Lecky must suffice: "We read of Christians bound in chains of red-hot iron, while the stench of the unconsumed bodies rose in a suffocating cloud to heaven; of others torn to the very bone by shells or books of iron; of holy virgins given over to the lust of gladiators, or the mercies of the panderer; of two hundred and twenty-seven sent on one occasion to the mines, each with one leg severed by a hot iron, and an eye scooped from the socket; of fires so slow that the victims writhed for hours in their agony; of tortures prolonged and varied through entire days. For the love of their divine Master, for the cause which they believed to be true, when one word would have freed them from their sufferings."

c. THE LORD'S SUPPER. On the night of his betrayal the Saviour instituted this Supper (Matt. 26:26-30), and from that day to this it has been observed wherever Christianity has gone. In fact, this institution has always been a part of the Christian religion. It is a significant fact that wherever this bloodless feast has been spread, there bloody sacrifices have ceased, and the sense of sin has been greatly intensified. When the sun rises, even men put out the other lights; and so when the sacrifice of Calvary is made, all minor sacrifices are discontinued.

What is the cause which produced this unique institution? It could not have been borrowed from Judaism, for it ignores the very heart of their memorial rite: the bloody sacrifice. It would also shock the Jews to have the Messiah represented in any sense as a sacrifice. Neither could it have come from Greek or Roman mythology, for there was nothing there to suggest it. And if Christ did not rise from the grave, the disciples would not observe it, for in that case it was the proclamation of a failure on the part of their Lord. But they did observe it, and wherever they went preaching "Jesus and the resurrection," this memorial feast was made a prominent part of the worship of the churches which they established.

But the strangest thing is yet to be said; viz., that this custom arose on the very spot, and immediately following the time, of the crucifixion. Ebrard says that "in the whole sphere of criticism there is no absurdity more uncritical than the idea that a rite which universally prevailed should have grown up accidentally and gradually, especially a rite of such marked peculiarity." But if we accept the New Testament account of the origin, purpose and promulgation, then all is simple and reasonable.

*d*. THE LORD'S DAY. From the beginning (Gen. 2:3) the Sabbath day was sacred. But it received an added sanctity when the Jews made it commemorative of their deliverance from Egyptian bondage (Deut. 5:15). Men naturally love and venerate ancient customs, often simply because they are ancient. But this day is not only hoary with age, but it commemorated two of the grandest events in the history of the world; yet it gives place to the Lord's Day, and becomes commemorative of two grander events: the new creation in Christ, and deliverance from sin. And this monument, like the Supper, began in Jerusalem, and just one week after the resurrection of the Christ. It would be absolutely impossible to induce the American people to observe the fourth of June instead of the fourth of July in commemoration of the Declaration of Independence; and it would be equally impossible to induce them to so observe the fourth of July, if no such Declaration ever took place. Yet the best people of the world for nineteen centuries have been observing the Lord's Day; have reared a monument in memory of an event which never occurred, if so be that Christ rose not. The tall white shaft, the highest monument in the world, which lifts its pinnacle into the clouds over Washington City, could never have been built if Washington had not been the savior of his people; neither could these two towering monuments, the Lord's Supper and the Lord's Day, have had their glorious history and sacred significance if Christ had not been "declared the Son of God with power by the resurrection from the dead" (Rom. 1:4).

It is said that Charlemagne at his own request was buried in a sitting posture, clothed in royal purple and ermine, with his crown on his head and his scepter in his hand. Years afterward the tomb was opened, but, alas! little was left of his imperial glory. The crown had fallen from his bleached brow, the scepter lay in the dust at his feet, and his royal robes had rotted about him. Not so with King Jesus. God had said that his body should not be left in the grave, and the holy One should not see corruption; and so on the morning of the third day he burst the bars of the tomb and came forth, bringing life and immortality to light through the gospel; and now lives and reigns and rules as the Lord of lords and the King of kings.

## REVIEW.

1. What is Paul's estimate of the resurrection?

2. Name five conceded facts concerning the Christ.

3. State the infidel position.

4. What three motives were used to corrupt their witnesses?

5. What story did these witnesses tell?

6. What would have been the result if they had presented the body of Jesus?

7. What is the Christian position?

8. State the trilemma, and discuss it.

9. What is the testimony of Greenleaf?

10. State the four points of corroborative testimony.

# VI.
# FAITH

# OUTLINE—CHAPTER VI.

1. What Is Faith?
2. How Is Faith Produced?
3. The Scope of Faith.
4. The Object of Faith.

# VI.

## FAITH.

Having established beyond a doubt the divinity of Christ, we next examine in detail the steps leading to salvation in him. We begin with the first step, faith.

**1. What Is Faith?** Paul answers this question as follows: "Now faith is the substance of things hoped for, the evidence of things not seen" (Heb. 11:1). This passage has suffered much at the hands of the scholarship of the church, and, like the poor woman of whom the Saviour tells us, who had suffered much at the hands of the physicians, it is generally unimproved by their treatment. Some of them say that it is not a definition, but a description, of faith. But as a definition, though about four hundred years old, it is not the best, and yet is not bad. The word rendered "substance" means that which stands under a structure, as its support or foundation. Hence, faith is the foundation on which things we hope for stand. The evidence of things not seen is the assurance that such things do exist. As we look forward to the beautiful temple of Hope, secure from every storm, and backward through the dim and shadowy past and see it, though invisible; or peer into the tangled present and behold God's hand leading and shielding at every step, we

101

realize something of what faith is. It is the mighty prop on which the past, the present and the future all rest.

But Edward Robinson's definition, in his great "Lexicon of the Greek New Testament," is better, and perhaps the best ever given. He says: "Faith is confidence as to things hoped for, conviction as to things not seen." According to this definition, faith has to do with two classes of things: things hoped for, and things unseen. As regards the unseen things, the word is wonderfully inclusive, and embraces everything in the past, the present and the future, of which we have no knowledge. Covering all such things, our faith is a "conviction," or assurance, that they do exist. As to the unseen things of the past we do not hope for them, but we do hope for many of the unseen things of the future. And when faith rests on these unseen objects of the future, then its second element is brought into action—confidence as to things hoped for. Aided by these two definitions, it would seem that we might have no doubt as to the correct meaning of this great word.

**2. How Is Faith Produced?** On this subject there has been much harmful teaching by theologians. It has been taught that man, being totally depraved, has no ability to believe, and therefore must wait for God's good time, when, in some miraculous way, he will give him faith. He has been told that he is as dead spiritually as Lazarus was physically, and that he can no more exercise a moral faculty without special divine aid than Lazarus could rise from the grave without the almighty power of the Saviour. The impression has been made that God has, as it were, an immense storage-battery in the heavens, and when he wills he touches it and flashes faith into the hearts of men much as we shock them with electricity. And so they are taught to pray for it, and expect it to come to them directly and irresistibly. If this is true, there is no such thing as human responsibility, and God can not be just and condemn man for unbelief.

But let us thank God that this baneful theory, now fast taking its flight from the haunts of men (Heaven hasten its going!), is false. If faith is the belief of testimony, then testimony must precede it, and man must possess the power to examine this testimony. The jury is not asked for a verdict without testimony. Their faith in the guilt or innocence of the prisoner comes not in some mysterious and independent manner, but according to the laws of the mind. And if one has not the power to exercise these mental powers, he is not eligible to jury service, and neither is he amenable to law. This is the clear, strong voice of reason; and, as is ever the case, it is in perfect accord with that of revelation.

Our faith in God did not come in this way. It is not the result of agonizing anxiety; of anxious prayer by ourselves and others; of strange dreams, visions or fleshly sensations, or anything of the kind. But when we were little children our mothers, in answer to our curious questions as to who made the sun and moon and stars and mountains and seas, opened the old family Bible and read its first verse to us: "In the beginning God created the heaven and the earth." And so it came from God's word. And our faith in Jesus came in the same way. These mothers read to us the story of his birth, his life, his death and his resurrection in the old Book, and we believed it.

Let us, therefore, have a few Scriptures in proof of this declaration.

"Neither pray I for these alone, but for them also who shall *believe on me through their word*" (John 17:20). The Saviour had been praying for his disciples, and now his great, loving heart looks forward and embraces the vast army of believers yet to come, who would believe on him through their word. And if our faith come not through their word—the gospel—we are not included in that prayer.

"Many other signs truly did Jesus, which are not written in this book, but these are written that *ye might believe that Jesus is the Christ,* the Son of God, and that believing *ye might have life through his name*" (John 20:30, 31). From this fine passage we get three important points: (*a*) Faith comes by hearing the gospel; (*b*) we are not to believe in dogmas, theories, speculations of men, etc., but in Christ; (*c*) the purpose of this faith is to give us life.

"Peter rose up and said, Men and brethren, ye know that a good while ago God made choice among us that the Gentiles *by my mouth should hear the word of the gospel, and believe"* (Acts 15:7). Language could not be clearer than this. If God chose that the Gentiles should hear the gospel and believe, then we should not expect faith independent of the gospel. But this Scripture is specially important because it is a part of the account of the conversion of Cornelius and his household, where there was a supernatural outpouring of the Holy Spirit. But Peter teaches that their faith was not the result of this miraculous gift of the Spirit, but of the Word which he preached to them.

"These were more noble than those in Thessalonica, in that they received the word with all readiness of mind, searching the scriptures daily, *whether these things were so.* Therefore many of them believed" (Acts 17:11, 12). The Thessalonians rejected the truth, and organized a rough mob to resist it. But the Bereans "received the word with all readiness of mind"; and they searched the Scriptures like miners search for gold; and this they did daily, giving it a continuous hearing. "Therefore many of them believed." Here we see the sure highways of faith: an honest heart, a candid hearing, and a searching investigation.

"So, then, *faith cometh by hearing, and hearing by the word of God"* (Rom. 10:17). This is so plain that it is hazardous to try to make it plainer. If it said that faith comes by feeling, or by the direct operation of the Spirit, we would so teach. But it says it comes by hearing the word of God, and this is the end of controversy to the man who believes.

**3. The Scope of Faith**

It stretches from the cradle to the grave, and is present at almost every step in the pilgrimage from the one to the other. It enlarges the horizon of the senses. If we were confined to the sphere of these, how circumscribed life would be. It would not be as broad as that of the animals about us, for their instincts are stronger than ours. But we can believe. In infancy, as we begin life's journey, it is by faith. Having little instinct, and no reason or experience, our only guide is faith in mother. She must teach us about nature and her stern laws—how fire will burn, water will drown, knives will cut, and poison will kill. And when we enter the schoolroom, faith in the teacher is our guide. But for this we could not learn the alphabet and multiplication table, and would never know the joys of literary life or experience the science of numbers. All the wealth of history, the beauty of the classics, and the heights and depths of philosophy would forever remain veiled to us. And in business life faith in our fellow-man is guide. It is the working principle in commercial life. The difference between the merchant prince and the petty trader is that one can go only so far as he can see, and the other sweeps out far beyond the boundaries of sight and sense and takes into account the relations of things, time, space, quality, quantity, seasons, races, latitudes. In a word, he makes the whole world contribute to his success. Ninety-nine per cent. of modern business is done through checks. We buy goods we have never seen, and sell them to men who are strangers to us.

In every bill of goods we buy, and in every draft we draw, we have to trust some one. If faith in the commercial world should be destroyed to-day, the wheels of traffic would stop and there would be universal bankruptcy in less than a year. It is the mutual faith of husband and wife that makes home possible. Cut the faith principle, and the home, and all society, would fall to pieces like beads when the string is broken. And but for faith, the state could not stand, and the nation would fall. Faith, therefore, is not an arbitrary thing, but it is rather that which restores man to the state of his primitive integrity.

But its scope includes much more than the practical things of every-day life. It is so vast that it almost staggers us when we contemplate it. With F. D. Power we can say: "Wider than the earth, broader than the sea, longer than all time, stretching into the eternal past and down through the eternal future, is the area of faith. By this we live in every age and clime, hold converse with men of every nation, and become contemporary with all generations. By this we know how worlds were made; how man came into being under the hand of his Maker; how the patriarchs, fathers and prophets lived and loved and suffered and died; how Christ was born of the Virgin Mary, taught, worked miracles, gave himself on the cross, came forth from the tomb, and ascended; how the gospel was preached, and men believed, repented and obeyed. Further, by faith we get the vision of unborn ages,

the ransomed coming to Zion with songs and everlasting joy on their heads, the new heavens and
the new earth wherein dwelleth righteousness.
'Faith is the evidence of things not seen.' Well
does Toplady call it the 'eye of the soul.' For, as
we stand by the deep chasm called the grave, it
bridges it, and in an instant we are in the land
where there are no graves, and the loved one is
ours once more. The astronomer from the observatory in his home looks into the upper depths
and sees thousands of shining worlds. He climbs
the mountain-top, and the number is multiplied.
Still unsatisfied, he goes into the world's greatest
observatory, and with its most powerful glass looks
again and finds them multiplied almost infinitely.
But has he seen all? No. But here he must stop,
not for want of worlds to see, but for lack of vision
to see them. But not so the Christian. When the
eye of sense fails him, by the lens of faith he
looks into the invisible things of God and revels
in the glory of heaven. Faith is glorified reason;
the imagination in its luminous hours."

**4. The Object of Faith**

What we believe is far more
important than how we believe.
The pipe through which the water
is brought is important, but not so much so as the
fountain from which it comes. If the fountain be
pure, then health and happiness are produced, but,
if impure, disease and death. It is not strange,
therefore, that the Bible holds up Jesus as the
object of faith. "And I, if I be lifted up from the
earth, will draw all men unto me" (John 12:32).

"As Moses lifted up the serpent in the wilderness, even so must the Son of man be lifted up; that whosoever believeth in him should not perish, but have eternal life. For God so loved the world that he gave his only begotten Son, that whosoever believeth in him should not perish, but have everlasting life" (John 3:14-16). "Let all the house of Israel know assuredly that God hath made that same Jesus whom ye have crucified, both Lord and Christ" (Acts 2:36). "Believe on the Lord Jesus Christ, and thou shalt be saved, and thy house" (Acts 16:31).

Man loves the concrete rather than the abstract, and he is never so strong as when the guiding principle of his life is embodied in a mighty personality. See this exemplified in the heroes who followed Wellington and Napoleon, and Lee and Grant, to danger and death rather than desert their leaders. By nature we are hero-worshipers. Doctrine, even though it come from God, and principles, though born in heaven, are never at their best until associated with a magnetic leader. This is why the Father has put everything spiritual in the Christ, so that Christ is Christianity and Christianity is Christ. "In him dwelleth all the fulness of the Godhead bodily, and ye are complete in him who is the head of all principality and power" (Col. 2:9, 10). And this is why the apostles in their preaching would know nothing but Jesus Christ and him crucified. And this is why the church under their ministry swept over Europe and Asia like an army with banners. And this is why our preaching has been so blessed of God. We have held up Christ instead of dogma, and preached the gospel rather than the philosophies, speculations and traditions of men.

Radium, the new substance now so much discussed in the scientific world, gives off light without heat, and thus symbolizes intellectual faith. There is often cold intellectuality without warmth, love or spiritual life. Light and heat should be combined. The pulpit and the pen should be knowledge aflame with love.

The faith that saves is not simply a mental assent. Paul once so preached before Felix that he trembled, but he was not saved. "The devils also believe and tremble," but they remain devils still. It must be a faith that leads to penitence, obedience, and a new life in the Saviour. As the sick man puts himself unreservedly in the hands of the physician, ready to do what he commands and refrain from what he forbids, so must the sin-sick soul surrender to the great Physician, and all will be well.

### REVIEW.

1. Give two definitions of faith.
2. How is faith produced?
3. Give five Scriptures bearing on this question.
4. What is the scope of faith?
5. Who is the object of faith?
6. Define the faith that saves.
7. Describe faith in the every-day life.
8. Describe faith in the hour of death.

# VII.
# REPENTANCE

# OUTLINE—CHAPTER VII.

1. What Is Repentance?
   a. Not Sorrow.
   b. Not Sorrow and Confession Combined.
   c. Not Godly Sorrow.
   d. Not Reformation.
   e. It Is Sorrow for Sin Resulting in Reformation.
2. Why Should Men Repent?
   a. Because God Commands It.
   b. Because of God's Goodness.
   c. Because of God's Warnings.
   d. Because the Impure Can Not Enter Heaven.
3. Fruits of Repentance.
   a. Confession of Sin.
   b. Prayer for Forgiveness.
   c. Restitution.
   d. New Life.

# VII.

## REPENTANCE.

Repentance, the second step on the way to pardon, has a prominent place in the gospel of the Saviour. It has been called the goddess of the erring, whose tearful voice is ever whispering: Salvation *from* sin, not *in* sin. And while we are struggling to answer this voice, we behold heaven, but we feel hell. Nothing is more difficult than true repentance. It is not so difficult to get men to believe. The testimony is so simple and strong that it convinces the honest and intelligent hearer in almost every case. Neither is it difficult to get the penitent believer to be baptized. When he fully surrenders to the Lord, he is anxious thus publicly to show his faith in him. The real difficulty is with repentance. It is no easy matter to induce the will, especially when it is in the wrong, to change. Sin so blinds the eye that it sees but dimly, and so muffles the ear that it hears imperfectly, and it so paralyzes the will that, like a palsied arm, it seems unable to act. Hence the power to so teach and preach as to make men repent is the power for which the teacher and preacher ought always to pray. But when we do repent, the reward is so rich that we forget the rough way over which we have had to travel. and the bitter cups we have had to drink, for it is our second innocence.

**1. What Is Repentance?**

*a.* IT IS NOT SORROW. Many emotional people seem to think that when the heart is convulsed and the tears flow freely, they have repented. But this is not necessarily true. Such emotions may be connected with genuine repentance, and they may not. Some men exercise repentance and never weep, and some weep and never repent. Sorrow is an essential element of repentance, but in itself it is not repentance. The alphabet is an essential part of an education, but he who only knows these twenty-six characters when he sees them, but does not know how to combine them into words and sentences, is not educated. Herod (Matt. 14: 1-11) made a hasty and wicked promise to the daughter of Herodias, and when he found that it involved the head of John the Baptist, he was "sorry." But he did not repent, but went forth in spite of his sorrow, and became a murderer in the sight of God and men.

*b.* IT IS NOT SORROW AND CONFESSION COMBINED. The sorrow of Judas so wrought upon him that he "brought again the thirty pieces of silver to the chief priests and elders, saying, I have sinned in that I have betrayed the innocent blood" (Matt. 27: 3, 4); but he did not repent. Instead, he "departed, and went and hanged himself." Here is confession coupled with sorrow, and still no repentance. Solomon says: "He that covereth his sins shall not prosper: but whoso confesseth and forsaketh them shall have mercy" (Prov. 28: 13).

Judas uncovered his sins, but he did not forsake

them. His was remorse rather than repentance.

*c*. IT IS NOT GODLY SORROW. "Now I rejoice, not that ye were made sorry, but that ye sorrowed to repentance; for ye were made sorry after a godly manner, that ye might receive damage by us in nothing. For godly sorrow worketh repentance to salvation not to be repented of; but the sorrow of the world worketh death" (2 Cor. 7:9, 10). If godly sorrow worketh repentance, it is not itself repentance, but its cause, and sustains to repentance the relationship of cause to effect.

*d*. IT IS NOT REFORMATION. There can be no repentance without reformation, but there may be reformation without repentance. A wicked and worthless young man might find his evil ways the only objection urged by the parents against his marriage to their daughter, and there might be temporary reformation in order to overcome this objection, but no repentance. In his case there would be no sorrow for sin—that sorrow that worketh repentance to salvation.

*e*. WHAT, THEN, IS REPENTANCE? If it is not sorrow; if it is not sorrow coupled with confession; if it is not godly sorrow; and if it is not reformation, what is it? It is sorrow for sin resulting in reformation of life; it is ceasing to do evil and learning to do well (Isa. 1:16, 17).

Let us see this definition in the light of two illustrations. The Ninevites were a wicked people, and God sent Jonah to preach to them. They heard him; they believed what he preached; they humbled themselves in the dust, fasted and put on sackcloth;

and they turned from their sins, and God forgave them (Matt. 12:41; Jonah 3:1-10).

The story of the prodigal son also is a lucid illustration. He left home and "spent his substance in riotous living"; he came down to wretchedness and want, and, while sorrowing over his sin, he determined to arise and go to his father and say unto him: "Father, I have sinned against heaven and before thee, and am no more worthy to be called thy son. Make me as one of thy hired servants. . . . And he arose and went" (Luke 15:11-24). His sorrow led to penitence, and his penitence ripened into reformation, and he was saved.

That the reader may know that this conclusion is in harmony with the best scholarship, we will hear Isaac Errett: "The Greek word translated 'repentance' indicates change—conversion. It imparts change of mind or disposition, and that, too, for the better. We have, indeed, more than one Greek word translated by this term 'repentance.' One of them indicates a change, whether for better or worse. But that word, expressing the will of God concerning us, uniformly in the New Testament denotes a change for the better. We are sometimes asked what is the difference between faith and repentance, since they are both expressive of change? We reply that the idea of change is not contained in the word 'faith,' although it usually implies a change; it is rather expressive of rest, of trust, of simple confidence. But the word 'repentance' is expressive of change. Faith respects that which is true; repentance, that which is right. Faith looks away from falsehood and error to the truth; repentance looks away from sin to righteousness and holiness."

**2. Why Men Should Repent**

*a.* BECAUSE GOD COMMANDS IT. "The times of this ignorance God winked at; but now commandeth all men every where to repent" (Acts 17: 30). There is but one safe thing to do with a commandment of God, and that is to obey it. It must not be resisted, ignored, neglected or trifled with. It is Jehovah who commands, and all his commandments are righteous, and he has the power to punish disobedience.

*b.* BECAUSE OF GOD'S GOODNESS. "Despisest thou the riches of his goodness and forbearance and longsuffering; not knowing that the goodness of God leadeth thee to repentance?" (Rom. 2:4). God is not only a King to command, and a Judge to inflict the penalty of disobedience, but he is a loving Father; yea, more, he is father and mother in one (Isa. 66:13), and his "goodness and forbearance and longsuffering" will be extended to all. Beecher says: "When a man undertakes to repent toward his fellow-man, it is repenting straight up a precipice; when he repents toward law, it is repenting in the crocodile's jaws; when he repents toward public sentiment, it is throwing himself into a thicket of brambles and thorns; and when he repents towards God, he repents toward all love and delicacy. God receives the soul as the sea the bather, to return it again, purer and whiter than he took it."

*c.* BECAUSE OF GOD'S WARNINGS. "Suppose ye
that these Galilæans were sinners above all the
Galilæans, because they suffered such things? I
tell you, Nay: but, except ye repent, ye shall all
likewise perish" (Luke 13:2, 3). All have sinned,
and, therefore, all must repent. The king on his
throne, the beggar at his gate, the mother and her
child, the father and his son, the murderer, the
slanderer, the pirate, the respectable, the poor wretch
covered with crime—all have sinned and come short
of the glory of God. But he warns all, and if we
will hear and heed, he forgives; if not, we perish.
Men often in hot passion punish, and then warn.
In the home—how sad that it is so—the parent's
blow is frequently first and the word of warning
follows. This is the rule with despots and tyrants,
especially when the rebellious subject is weak. They
crush him first and reason with him later. There is
no previous warning and no time for repentance.
Not so with our God. He will not cut down the
fruitless tree that cumbereth the ground, until it
has been dug about and dunged (Luke 13:8); he
will not drown a wicked world until it is fully
warned of the impending doom; Sodom shall not
perish until righteous Lot has lived within her
borders; Nineveh shall not fall until Jonah has
preached in her streets; Babylon shall not be
crushed till Daniel has lived in her midst; and Jerusalem shall not be ground under the tyrant's heel
until she has received a thousand warnings. How
many warnings from the Bible, from the pulpit and
press, from sickness and sorrow, and from in-

numerable other sources, have been received by all, and how shall we escape if we heed them not?

*d.* BECAUSE THE IMPURE CAN NOT ENTER HEAVEN. "Who shall ascend into the hill of the Lord? or who shall stand in his holy place? He that hath clean hands and a pure heart" (Ps. 24: 3, 4); "Blessed are the pure in heart: for they shall see [enjoy] God" (Matt. 5:8). Heaven is a place of purity, and none but the pure can be happy there. If the ignorant are ill at ease among the learned, and the coarse among the refined, how could the sinner, unforgiven, be happy among the redeemed? If by almighty power the Lord should suddenly transfer the profligate, the blasphemer and the drunkard to heaven without repentance, heaven would be hell to them, and they would struggle to escape from its pure atmosphere. As the diseased eye is pained by the light, so the impure in heart would flee from God. Heaven is a prepared place for a prepared people.

**3. Fruits of Repentance** John, evidently with doubt in his mind as to the purity of purpose of some who came to be baptized, called upon them to "bring forth fruits meet for repentance" (Matt. 3:8). This was right; for genuine repentance, like a good tree, will always bear good fruit. What are some of these fruits?

*a.* CONFESSING SIN. "Wash me thoroughly from mine iniquity, and cleanse me from my sin; for I acknowledge my transgressions, and my sin is ever before me" (Ps. 51:3, 4). "If we confess our sins, he is faithful and just to forgive us our

sins, and to cleanse us from all unrighteousness"
(1 John 1:9). "Father, I have sinned against
heaven and in thy sight, and am no more worthy
to be called thy son" (Luke 15:21). Every one
who truly repents is anxious to imitate the penitent
prodigal and seek forgiveness in humble confession
of sin. Until we are willing to do this, it is clear
that we do not appreciate the heinous character of
sin.

*b.* PRAYER FOR FORGIVENESS. "And the publican,
standing afar off, would not lift up so much as his
eyes unto heaven, but smote upon his breast, saying,
God be merciful to me a sinner" (Luke 18:13).
The sight of sin always brings the soul to its knees.
When a child which loves its mother discovers that
it has broken her commandments and grieved her
heart, it instinctively seeks her presence and prays
her forgiveness. And how can the mother heart
refuse? It is said of the big-hearted Lincoln that
he issued standing orders for the admission of
every messenger who sought his aid in saving a
life. However great the throng who waited on
him, such a messenger was admitted first. And
regardless of the standing of those who sought an
audience—though they were Senators, Congressmen,
Cabinet officers, foreign representatives, and mil-
lionaires—all had to wait on him who sought the
life of some condemned man. "If ye then, being
evil, know how to give good gifts unto your children, how much more shall your Father which is
in heaven give good gifts to them that ask him?"
(Matt. 7:11).

*c.* RESTITUTION. No amount of profession and emotion and agony will avail without restitution, provided restitution be within our power. In Matt. 5:23, 24 the Saviour teaches that we are to right our wrongs against man before we offer sacrifice to God: "Therefore if thou bring thy gift to the altar, and there rememberest that thy brother hath aught against thee; leave there thy gift before the altar, and go thy way; first be reconciled to thy brother, and then come and offer thy gift." Sin-offerings without repentance are worthless, but not more so than repentance without sin-offerings. When we sin against man we sin against God, and we must first be reconciled to man before God will hear us. A man sins against the child of his neighbor. How can the matter be adjusted? He must first undo the wrong to the child before he can expect the forgiveness of the father. And man is God's child. The liar, therefore, must confess and correct his falsehood, the thief must restore the stolen goods, the fraudulent man must disgorge, and the hypocrite must reform, before we may expect the forgiveness of the Father. Let Zacchæus be our example (Luke 19:8).

*d.* A NEW LIFE. "Therefore if any man be in Christ, he is a new creature: old things are passed away; behold, all things are become new" (2 Cor. 5:17). Repentance is often shallow and inadequate. It is like that of the little girl who was punished for her naughtiness. At night, before being tucked away in bed, she prayed to God: "O God, please make me good, not real good, but just good enough

so I won't have to be whipped." F. D. Power puts
this point most forcibly: "There must be a godly
walk and conversation. The man who formerly
was a liar will now be known far and wide as a
truthful man. The man given to dishonest practices will now show himself upright and reliable in
all his transactions. The man who aforetime was
profane, impious, unjust, inhuman, given to ungod-
liness and worldly lust, now lives soberly, right-
eously and godly. The man who once, like the
prodigal, reveled in impurity and drunkenness, is
now proving himself chaste and temperate. The
soul that cared formerly only for the mad whirl of
pleasure and worldliness finds delight now in things
spiritual and divine. The world sees the reformation is genuine." Thus may we rise on stepping-
stones of our dead selves to higher and holier
things. And in this there is nothing base nor bitter.
It is only good rising out of evil. It is the resurrection of purity from the grave of lust. It is darkness fleeing before the dawn. It is weakness clothing itself with the strength of Jehovah. It is the
prisoner, freed from shackles, bolts and bars, step-
ping forth a free man. As the water-lily, white and
pure, and admired by all, rises from the black filth
of the lake or bog, so the sweet flower of repentance springs from the bitter pangs of remembered
wrongs, and "is only the soul blossoming back to
its better nature."

Beecher puts the case forcefully and beautifully:
"Men look upon repentance and humiliation before
God very much as they do upon a voyage to the

North Pole. Every single league, as they advance toward the Arctic region, they leave more and more behind them greenness, and fruits and warmth, and civilization, and find themselves more and more in the midst of sterility, barrenness, ice and barbarism. Men think that to go to God is dreary and desolate in the extreme. It is not! The sinner is the Esquimaux! He lives in ice and burrows underground, and is but little better than a beast. But if by any means he becomes fired with a conception of a better clime, and, leaving his hibernating quarters, he takes the ship of Repentance and sails toward the Torrid Zone, at every league he is surprised by the new forms of vegetation. He has seen oak-trees only about as high as his knee. Not long after he sets out on his voyage, he is astonished to see them as high as his head. As he draws near the tropics, he is lost in wonder and ecstasy to see them lifting themselves far above him in the air. And with what satisfaction does he compare the delightful home he has found with the miserable one he left."

REVIEW.

1. Is it difficult to exercise true repentance?

2. Define repentance.

3. Give two Bible examples of repentance.

4. What does Errett say as to the words "repentance" and "faith"?

5. Give four reasons why we should repent.

6. State four fruits of repentance.

7. Quote Power on the subject.

8. Give Beecher's illustration.

# VIII.
# CONVERSION

# OUTLINE—CHAPTER VIII.

1. CLEARING THE GROUND.
    a. ALL HEAR, BUT ALL ARE NOT SAVED.
    b. MEN DEAD IN SIN CAN NOT ACT OF
        THEMSELVES.
    c. A BIBLE EXAMPLE.
2. FILING OBJECTIONS.
    a. IT TURNS ATTENTION FROM THE GOS-
        PEL.
    b. IT DESTROYS HUMAN RESPONSIBILITY.
    c. IT MAKES GOD A CRUEL MONSTER.
    d. IT MAKES INFIDELS.
3. WHAT IS CONVERSION?
4. AIM AND END OF CONVERSION.

# VIII.

## CONVERSION.

But for the confusion and uncertainty created by the theologians, the searcher after truth, with his heart purified by faith and his life purified by repentance, would at once be baptized and enter fully into the Christian life. But the air is full of questions about conversion, change of heart, and the like, and he is afraid that he is not fit for baptism; and so postpones it for the present, that he may look into these questions. He begins with the study of conversion.

This is a question of the greatest possible importance to every one, and it should be carefully studied.

**1. Clearing the Ground**
But, in order to such study, some difficulties must be removed. During the time of the apostles, and for two hundred years later, these difficulties did not exist. The gospel, as "the power of God unto salvation" (Rom. 1:16), was preached and men were saved. Near the close of the fourth century Satan sowed the seed of speculative theology, and the trouble began. Augustine espoused it, and it soon became a power for evil. He taught that, because of the fall of Adam, all, even infants, were so depraved as to destroy the human will and leave them the helpless servants of sin. This

9 127

being true, conversion was necessarily miraculous, God's power in it being irresistible, and this power was exerted only on the elect. At first thought it seems incredible that such a theory could be accepted by any one. But many like the mysterious, especially in religion. Enshroud a subject in fog, and let it stand like a mountain wrapped in mist, half revealed and half concealed, and their imaginations are impressed, and the heart is filled with holy (?) awe. Then the priest has his feast.

*a*. ALL MEN HEAR THE GOSPEL, BUT ALL ARE NOT SAVED; HENCE THIS MIRACULOUS POWER IS EXERTED IN BEHALF OF SOME, AND WITHHELD FROM OTHERS. The Saviour, in the parable of the sower (Matt. 13:1-9, 18-23), fully explains this matter. Some seed fell on the wayside, some on stony ground, some among thorns, and some on good ground. In some cases there was no fruit, in others it was slight, and in the last an abundant harvest. This was not because a miraculous power was sometimes exerted, and sometimes withheld, but because of variety in soil and circumstances. The seed, which is the word of God (Luke 8:11), was the same in each case, but the soil, which is the human heart, was not. This explanation, simple, sound and philosophical, should commend itself to all.

*b*. SINNERS ARE DEAD IN SIN, AND, BEING DEAD, IT REQUIRES MIRACULOUS POWER TO BRING THEM BACK TO LIFE. "How shall we that are dead to sin live any longer therein?" (Eph. 2:1).

Here the two words "dead" and "live" are applied to the same individual, showing that he was dead in 'one sense and alive in another. If, then, when Christians are dead "to" sin, they are able still to do wrong, sinners, when dead "in" sin, are able to do right. To interpret these and kindred passages so as to teach that one is so dead that he can not hear, understand or obey the gospel is to treat a figure of rhetoric as if it were a literal statement of truth. Let us see the absurdity of this in another Pauline passage: "Awake thou that sleepest, and arise from the dead, and Christ shall give thee light" (Eph. 5:14). Death here is not absolute, and does not imply that the dead are unable to hear the cry, to awake, or to rise from the dead. The fact is that total depravity, except in rare cases (Eph. 4:19), is a myth of man's theology, and not the teaching of the Bible. "Evil men and seducers shall wax worse and worse, deceiving and being deceived" (2 Tim. 3:13). If men are totally depraved, it is impossible for them to wax worse. We all possess both good and evil (Rom. 7:21-23), and salvation is the development of the good, and damnation is the development of the evil. None are so good but that they may become better, and few are so bad that they may not become worse.

c. A BIBLE EXAMPLE. The case of Lydia (Acts 16:14, 15) is confidently relied on as proof of this theory. Luke says that Paul preached to her, and that the Lord "opened" her heart, which is regarded as proof that it was so bad that miraculous power was essential to her conversion. But this is a slander on a good woman, for there is no proof that her heart was so bad that it could not be opened by ordinary means. Here is another example of figurative speech. The word "heart" is compared to something narrow or contracted, or closed up entirely, and needed to be expanded or opened. The trouble with Lydia's heart was not that she was totally depraved—far from it—but as a Jewish worshiper she believed that the Messiah would restore the old Davidic throne, and bring back the lost glory of the children of Abraham. She had no conception of the world-wideness of his mission. Thus was her heart contracted, and it needed opening. Imagine a close-fisted, stingy man, able but unwilling to give of his means. But on a certain occasion a preacher makes an appeal for a worthy cause, and it reaches his contracted heart and expands it so that he responds liberally. In this case it might be said that his heart was opened by the preacher. But surely it would not be claimed that a miracle was wrought. None was needed. The truth only entered, and the heart was expanded and the purse was opened. Even so when the gospel—a gospel not for the Jew only, but for all men—entered Lydia's heart, it was opened as was the heart of Peter in the house of Cornelius, and she received it with joy.

Let us note a few of the elements of this woman's character, and see that it was not bad: She was, like Cornelius, a worshiper of God, and his prayers and alms were acceptable to God.

When called away from home she took her religion with her—a mighty proof of its genuineness. She closed her store on the Sabbath day, regardless of the fact that her rivals kept theirs open—another weighty proof of genuine conviction. Though her people seemed too poor to have a fashionable place of worship, she was not ashamed of them, but worshiped God with them in an open-air meeting by the river-side. And though they seemed not to have a man among them, she was loyal to her God. Do these facts indicate a bad woman? If you know one such to-day, do you not point to her as a model Christian?

But, being a Jewish worshiper, her heart was narrow. It was contracted by the prejudices of that bigoted people. But, being an honest heart, it received the large, new truth which Paul preached, and thus it was "opened," expanded, enlarged, just as multitudes of similar hearts are being opened every day. The gospel in such a heart is like the sun on a rosebud. It opens it, and enlarges and beautifies it, and causes it to send forth its sweet incense into the world. No miracle is necessary. Nature's laws are all that is needed.

**2. Filing Objections** Having removed the main props under this theory, we next consider some serious objections to it.

*a.* IT TURNS ATTENTION AWAY FROM THE GOSPEL. "I am not ashamed of the gospel of Christ, for it is the power of God unto salvation to every one that believeth" (Rom. 1:16). If the gospel is

God's power to save, any theory of conversion which turns the attention of the unsaved away from it, is false. This theory does so teach, and hence it is false. God uses no superfluous means. If one life-boat will save, why send two? If the gospel is "the power of God unto salvation," why another power? Note the fact that it is not a power—one of two, or many powers—but it is *the* power: the one sole and all-sufficient power to save.

*b.* IT DESTROYS HUMAN RESPONSIBILITY. If miracle is essential to conversion, and if God only can work miracles, then man is not responsible for his sin. "Trust God and keep your power dry," said Cromwell; not, "Trust God to keep your powder dry."

*c.* IT MAKES GOD A CRUEL MONSTER. The Bible teaches that he is our Father, and that he loves us with an infinite love. But this theory makes him a heartless monster, cruel and arbitrary. He tantalizes all with the offer of salvation, but refuses to exert the necessary power in the case of many, and thus mocks them in their misery, and trifles with them when the soul's eternal interests are involved. If you, a father, had two boys, weary and hungry, would you spread a tempting feast before them, knowing that they could not reach it without special help from you, and yet extend the help to one and withhold it from the other? If so, you are a merciless monster, and deserve, as you would receive, the execration of all men. Any theory which so represents God, must be wrong.

*d.* IT MAKES INFIDELS. Thoughtful people, seek-

ing salvation, hear such preaching, turn from it
with instinctive disgust, and say that it can not
be the teaching of a just and loving God, and,
knowing nothing better, they drift out into the cold
sea of infidelity. Thousands of this class, many of
them the brainiest and best, are in our midst to-day.
Many of them do not turn from God at once, but
go to the mourners' bench, and wait and watch
and pray for this special power. It does not come,
and they finally turn back to their former lives with
the deepest conviction that the whole thing is a
farce, or that God is a respecter of persons. I speak
both from wide observation and painful experience.

We are now ready to raise the question:

**3. What Is Con-** Conversion is turning. A
**version?** traveler discovers that he is on
the wrong road. He halts, turns
about, and changes his course. So, the sinner, dis-
covering that he is on the road to ruin, pauses, faces
about and begins his march over the narrow road
which leads to life. Moody's definition is good:
"Halt! Right about face! Forward, march!" But
the Saviour's is better: The story of the prodigal
son. He is plunging downward to death. The
heavy hand of affliction is laid upon him. He
pauses, realizes his deep degradation, repents,
resolves to do better, and at once puts his resolu-
tion into effect, and returns to his father and is
forgiven.

The three thousand Jews at Pentecost, with
hands stained in the blood of the Saviour, are
arrested by Peter's sermon. They see their awful

guilt, and cry out for help. The preacher tells them what to do. And the same day they change their course and enter the kingdom of God. Paul, breathing out threatenings and slaughter against the disciples of Christ, and having destroyed the church in Jerusalem, and about to repeat this destruction in Damascus, is arrested in his mad career, and made to see his sin; when suddenly his mighty life, with its measureless influence, is given to God. And so of the eunuch, Lydia, the jailer, and multitudes of others in the Book of Acts; they hear, they halt, they turn about, are converted and saved. Could anything be simpler? Can not a child understand it? Why, then, so much confusion about it? There can be but one answer: it is because of the mist and fog with which the speculative theologians have surrounded it. Brush this away by the breath of the pure gospel, and there is not a responsible mortal beneath the stars who can not understand it.

In the process of conversion let it never be forgotten that man, of his own accord, does the turning. He is not a machine, turned to the right or left, and driven backward or forward, by some power other than his own; but he is a man in the image of God and endowed with the power of choice, and he turns to the right or left, and moves forward or backward, according to his own volition. So fearfully and wonderfully made is he that he can look up into the face of God and say, "I will" or "I will not," and Jehovah respects his decision. His heart is his castle, and no man, and no angel, and not even his Maker, has the right to enter without his permission. "O Jerusalem, Jerusalem, thou that killest the prophets, and stonest them which are sent unto thee, how often would I have gathered thy children together, even as a hen gathereth her chickens under her wings, and ye would not!" (Matt. 23:37). "Behold, I stand at the door, and knock: if any man hear my voice, and open the door, I will come in to him, and will sup with him, and he with me" (Rev. 3:20). He was active in his degeneration, and he must be active in his regeneration. Of his own will he turned away from God, and of his own will he must come back to him.

Proof of this proposition is found in the fact that the original for "conversion" occurs in the New Testament thirty-nine times, and in every case except one (the Revised Version) the ripe product of the scholarship of both the Old and New Worlds renders it "turn" (active) and not "be turned" (passive). The same verb, without the preposition, occurs eighteen times, and in every case it is active. Is it not time that we drop the old and false phrase "be converted," and take up the new and true one, "turn"?

Every Bible conversion has in it three great changes—a change of heart, a change of life and a change of state. And God has provided three agencies to produce these changes. Faith changes the heart, repentance changes the life, and baptism changes the state or relationship. This order can not be reversed.

The state can not be changed first, and then the life and heart. The heart is the beginning-place.

There can be no repentance, or change in life, until we believe we have done wrong. And when we do so believe, the repentance naturally follows. And after the change in heart and life, and never before, are we to be baptized, which changes the relationship. The marriage ceremony illustrates this well. In every true marriage these three distinct steps take place. Faith, ripening into loving confidence and trust, changes the hearts. Their lives are changed, not by repentance, it is true, but they are changed. Their conduct toward each other, and toward others, is not what it once was; and yet they are not married. But when the marriage ceremony is performed, their relationship is changed. Before the ceremony, despite the changes already experienced, they were in the single state, and afterward they were in the married state. Baptism is the marriage ceremony by which the penitent soul is made part of the bride of Christ.

**4. The Aim and End of Conversion**  "If any man be in Christ Jesus, he is a new creature: old things are passed away; behold, all things are become new" (2 Cor. 5: 17). The servant-girl, when asked for proof of her conversion, gave the true answer: "I now sweep under the rugs." Before her conversion she had been an "eye-servant," taking advantage of her mistress, but now she is honest. Her conversion did not impart any new faculties to the soul, for they were not needed; but it revolutionized her life by turning these faculties into a new channel. She thought, desired, loved and hated as before, but the subjects of her thought, desire, love and hatred are changed. Conversion is like refitting an old ship and employing it in the service of a new and better master. Christ takes possession of the ship and puts on a new pilot and new compass, and throws overboard everything that is evil, and fills her with a better cargo, and turns her toward heaven. It is the same ship, but her course is changed.

### REVIEW.

1. Was conversion a simple subject in New Testament times?

2. How was it mystified?

3. How answer the three arguments on depravity?

4. Name four objections to the theory.

5. Define conversion.

6. Is man active or passive in conversion?

7. What three changes in conversion?

8. What is the great purpose of conversion?

# IX.
# CHANGE OF HEART

# OUTLINE—CHAPTER IX.

1. WHAT IS THE HEART?
   *a.* IT BELIEVES.
   *b.* IT LOVES.
   *c.* IT WILLS.
   *d.* IT CONDEMNS.
2. HOW IS THE HEART CHANGED?
   *a.* THE INTELLECT BY TESTIMONY.
   *b.* THE AFFECTIONS BY LOVELINESS.
   *c.* THE WILL BY MOTIVES.
   *d.* THE CONSCIENCE BY RIGHT-DOING.
3. AN EXAMPLE.

## Change of Heart.

Perhaps there is no question connected with Christianity around which more mist is found than the question of "'change of heart"; and possibly not one of them so little deserves this misty environment.

1. **What Is the Heart?** Before inquiring how the heart is changed, let us know what it is. It can not be the fleshly heart located in the left breast, for it is the same before and after conversion. It is no more changed than the hand or foot.

Let us ascertain what the heart is, by what it does. If a man shoes horses, he is a blacksmith; if he sells goods, he is a merchant; if he practices law, he is a lawyer. Now, if we can find what the heart does, we can safely decide what the heart is. What does it do? The word "heart" occurs many times in the Bible, and yet all these passages are capable of a fourfold classification, showing that the heart does four things.

*a.* It Believes. "For this people's heart is waxed gross, their ears are dull of hearing, and their eyes have they closed; lest they should see with their eyes, and hear with their ears, and should understand with their heart" (Matt. 13: 15). "And immediately when Jesus perceived in his spirit that they so reasoned within themselves, he said unto them, Why reason ye these things in mouth confession is made unto salvation" (Rom. 10: 10). These Scriptures teach that the heart understands, reasons and believes. Let us, for the present, separate these faculties from the will, the emotions, etc., and understand them to include simply the power to examine testimony and render verdicts.

*b.* It Loves. "So Absalom stole the hearts of the men of Israel" (2 Sam. 15:6). By examining the context it will be seen that Absalom was a modern-day politician. The handsome young prince, with "chariots" and horses, and "fifty men to run before him," was found on the highway pouring out sympathy for the "dear people"; and when one came near to do him "obeisance, he put forth his hand, and kissed him." Thus he found their affections, or stole their hearts. "Master, which is the greatest commandment in the law? Jesus said unto him, Thou shalt love the Lord thy God with all thy heart, and with all thy soul, and with all thy mind" (Matt. 22:36). In this passage the heart is meant specially to include the affections.

*c.* It Wills. "Nevertheless he that standeth stedfast in his heart, having no necessity, but hath power over his own will, and hath so decreed in his own heart that he will keep his virgin, doeth well" (1 Cor. 7:37). "Every man according as he purposeth in his heart, so let him give; not grudgingly, or of necessity: for God loveth a cheerful giver" (2 Cor. 9:7). Here it is seen that, in addition to faith and affections, the heart includes the will.

*d.* IT CONDEMNS. "Let us draw near with a true heart in full assurance of faith, having our hearts sprinkled from an evil conscience, and our bodies washed with pure water" (Heb. 10:22). "For if our heart condemn us, God is greater than our heart, and knoweth all things" (1 John 3:20). A fourth element, the conscience, the power that condemns when we do wrong, is now added to the heart.

Having now learned from the Book that the heart includes the intellect—the reasoning power; the affections—the power to love; the will—the great drive-wheels of humanity, and the conscience —the inner monitor, which cheers us when in the right, and chides us when in the wrong—we are able to decide as to what it is. It embraces the "inner man"—everything except the flesh and blood —and includes all that is immortal in man. It sweeps out natures from their loftiest heights to their deepest depths, and includes the whole of the spiritual in its ample scope.

**2. How is the Heart Changed?** While answering this question, let us remember that we have not two sets of faculties, as some seem to think, one for religion, and the other for the things of the world. The same powers used in business and in intellectual and moral matters are to be used in religion. And when we see how they are used in these things, we can understand their use in spiritual matters.

10

*a.* THE INTELLECT IS CHANGED BY TESTIMONY. You are on a jury, and the lawyer wishes so to change your mind that you will render a verdict in favor of his client. How does he proceed? He submits testimony, and asks you to examine it. Is there any other reasonable and honorable way to proceed? If not, and man having but one set of mental faculties, is it rational to expect God to proceed in a different way when he wants the mind changed? Suppose the lawyer should command you to believe his client innocent, but furnish no proof; or suppose he should earnestly, tenderly and eloquently pray for the change in your heart, and should have others pray for you, and should induce you to pray, what would you think of him? You would answer: "The man is either himself deceived—does not know the nature of man—or he thinks I do not, and he is trying to deceive me. I can not believe without testimony." Certainly not. Neither can you believe in God and Christ without testimony, hence they have piled it about you, mountain high, and made it so clear that the wayfaring man, though a fool, shall not err therein.

*b.* THE AFFECTIONS ARE CHANGED BY LOVELI-NESS. We instinctively love the lovely A vine is prostrate on the ground. You want it to rise, and you speak to it: "Little vine, get up out of the dust, so that you may breathe the sweet, pure atmosphere of heaven." It can not do it. Its tendrils are reaching everywhere for a support by which to rise. You see this, and place the trellis within reach, and it begins to climb toward the

sun. It needs no command or exhortation, but a
trellis. The babe, cooing on its mother's bosom,
needs not to be told to love her. The heart tendrils
will fasten themselves about her—if she is lovely.
You need not try to make the world love you.
Only be lovely and the world will do the rest. And
so it is in our religious nature. And when Christ,
the fairest among ten thousand and the one altogether lovely, is presented to the heart, it clasps its
arm about the cross, and is lifted up to God. No
wonder the Master said: "And I, if I be lifted up
from the earth, will draw all men unto me" (John
12:32); and no wonder that Paul, the prince of
preachers, said: "I determined not to know anything among you, save Jesus Christ and him crucified" (1 Cor. 2:2).

c. THE WILL IS CHANGED BY MOTIVES. A man
woos and wins the heart of a lovely woman, and he
solemnly vows to be a true husband. But the
vows are broken, and her heart is crushed. The
light from her eye goes out; the tint fades from
the cheek, and her laughter is changed to sobs and
sighs. With every hope blasted, and surrounded by
the ruins of all that she once held dear, and with
her little ones about her, she cries in the depths of
her desolate heart, not with her lips: "Precious
children, but for you I would launch myself into
awful eternity. Your father, once so good and
true, has become a wreck—a helpless, hopeless
wreck—and I am desolate indeed." This man is
your friend; and you would rescue him, and light
again with joy and love that little cottage home.

He loves his wife and children; he knows his duty; and in his better moments he desires to be to them again what he once was—a true husband and father. But, oh, how weak! His will power is shattered, and he is no longer a match for the tempter.

What does he need? How can you rescue him? His mind does not need changing, and his affections do not need rekindling. But his will power needs to be aroused. How shall this be done? You tell him of his sorrowing wife and precious children, and of their love for him and need of him. And as you plead with him he weeps and despises himself as a covenant-breaker and a weakling. He clenches his teeth, bites his lips, and, with almost superhuman effort, once more rallies his broken powers, sends up a petition to God for help, and, like the prodigal, says, "I will arise!" And he does, in the strength of Jehovah, rise and become a man again. How was it done? The motives connected with wife and babies, coupled with help from on high, enabled him to rise. And so, when the Father would change our wills and nerve us for life's great battles, he presents motives embracing every good thing in this life and in the life to come—motives high as heaven, deep as hell, broad as the universe, pure as Jesus, and strong and lasting as the pillars of the throne of glory.

*d.* THE CONSCIENCE IS CHANGED BY RIGHT-DOING. A child disobeys mother and is unhappy. And conscience, with a scourge of small cords, lashes the little one into an agony. With swollen eyes she tosses on her bed, for the sweet angel,

Sleep, refuses to come. The guilty bosom, like the boiling sea, is tumbling, rolling and groaning under the mad chastening of the storm.

What is her trouble? and how shall it be remedied? Her trouble is wrong-doing, and its only cure is right-doing. Let her steal up to mamma's side, throw her arms about her neck, beg her forgiveness, while she promises to be a better girl, and all will be well. The dark clouds will vanish, the angry waves will become calm, the fearful thunders will hush, the fierce lightnings will cease, and the sunlight of sweet peace will once more fill the soul.

When the conscience of Zacchæus condemned him, he promised to undo the wrong by bestowing half his goods upon the poor, and by restoring four-fold for all his fraudulent gains, and peace came to his heart and home. When the prodigal son fully realized his sin, he retraced his steps, and found peace and pardon and plenty awaiting his return. And thus it must· ever be. When we sin against God or man, the conscience, if not dead, will chide, and continue to chide until, so far as we are able, we undo the wrong.

Would you have your heart changed? Remember its importance. It is the hinge on which eternal destinies turn. No change of heart means no peace of soul on earth, and no home in heaven. Its importance can not be exaggerated.

**3. An Example** A young woman was intensely interested in her salvation, and she became so wrought up over the question of a change of heart that her friends feared for the safety of her mind. Many attempts were made to meet her difficulty, but all failed. Finally, an old preacher, who had no diploma or eccelsiastical titles, but a man of rugged common sense, who knew his Bible and humanity, came that way. The parents besought him to help their darling daughter. He gladly made the attempt. And he soon learned that her trouble grew out of confusion of thought as to a change of heart. She had no conception as to what the heart was, and hence was totally ignorant as to how it was changed. She had been taught that every conversion was the result of miraculous power, and she was waiting and praying for God to put forth that power and save her soul. But, being a woman of good mind, she soon learned the way of the Lord more perfectly. He asked her if she believed in God and Christ and the Bible, and she said she did. "Well," said he, "that part of the mind which believes is all right. You do not want it changed, for then you would no longer believe in your Creator, Saviour and their Book." She saw the point, and agreed with her new preacher.

He then asked if she loved God, Christ, the Bible, and everything good; and was assured that she did. "Then," said the preacher, "you do not want that part of the heart which loves—the affections—changed, for then you would hate these things." Again she agreed with him, and urged him to go on with his instructions.

He next asked as to her purpose in life: had she determined to be a Christian? She answered that that was her supreme purpose. "Then, your will needs no change," he said. "Your purpose is pure and heavenward, and it would be ruinous to change it." Once more she grasped his clear logic, and begged him to go on.

He now asked if her conscience gave her trouble, and was told that it almost drove her wild. "The only way to stop its lashings," said he, "is to undo the wrongs of the past as far as possible, and faithfully do the right in the future." She confessed her Saviour, and was baptized, and became a bright and shining light in the church. The conscience, the only section of the heart in rebellion, was changed, and she was at peace.

How is it with you? If your faith and affections and purposes are all pointing to God, as is true in many cases, and yet you are not happy, follow the example of this girl, and your heart will also be flooded and sweetened with the joys of heaven.

### REVIEW.

1. How can we tell what the heart is?
2. What four things does the heart do?
3. How is the intellect changed?
4. How are the affections changed?
5. How is the will changed?
6. How is the conscience changed?
7. Give an example illustrative of the change.

# X.

# THE CONFESSION

# OUTLINE—CHAPTER X.

1. Origin of the Confession.
2. Scope of the Confession.
   - *a.* "Thou art the Christ."
   - *b.* "The Son."
   - *c.* "Of the Living God."
3. The Confession and Baptism.
4. Why We Should Make the Confession.
   - *a.* For Our Own Good.
   - *b.* For the Good of Others.
   - *c.* For the Good of Christ.

# X.

## The Confession.

Now that the atmosphere about conversion, change of heart, etc., has been cleared up, we are ready to consider the question of the confession.

Confession and baptism are so intimately related that a Scriptural discussion of the one involves the other. They are related to each other as sorrow and repentance, as love and marriage. There may be sorrow without repentance, and there may be love without marriage; but there can be no repentance without sorrow, and no marriage without love. Sorrow and love precede repentance and marriage, and make them possible. And so is confession related to baptism, and hence it should be studied in connection with that ordinance. But for our present purpose it is probably best, so far as possible, to study it as a distinct theme.

**1. Origin of the Confession**

When Christ appeared among men they formed different opinions regarding him, just as they do to-day. Some thought him good, and others thought him bad; some said he was human, and others said he was divine; some thought him a teacher sent of God, and others that he was a deceiver of the people, and so they would express themselves. One would say, "I believe he is the Messiah;" another, "I believe he is a prophet;" and still another, "I believe he is an impostor." Thus a line was drawn, and his enemies agreed "that if any did confess that he was the Christ, he should be put out of the synagogue" (John 9:22). The Saviour accepted the test and said: "He that confesses me before men, him will I confess before my Father in heaven; but he that denies me before men, him will I deny before my Father in heaven" (Matt. 10:32, 33). Thus the confession, as regards men, originated naturally, and served to identify the followers of Christ; and on this account it became associated with baptism, the ordinance in which the sinner in symbol was separated from the service of Satan and dedicated to the service of God.

Later in the Master's ministry the confession received an emphasis which gave to it the greatest possible importance. Benjamin Franklin made one of the most daring and far-reaching experiments ever made by man. A cluster of clouds hung over his head, and he gazed wistfully upon them, longing for light on a scientific question. Finally he let fly a paper kite with a metallic chain attached. He waited, watched and wondered, and finally applied his knuckles to the chain, and the sparks of the wild lightning played about him; and had the stream been a little stronger, the bold philosopher would have died on the spot. And so clouds of opinions filled the heavens about the Saviour. Some said he was John the Baptist; some, that he was Elijah; others, that he was Jeremiah; and many, that he was one of the prophets. Everything was vague, hazy and misty, and, wanting something definite, he sent out two questions—kite-like—and they brought back light and truth of infinitely more value than that secured by Franklin. "Whom do men say that I, the Son of man, am?" (Matt. 16:13). And the answer came that he was some great personage ranking with the old heroes and prophets of the past. Another question quickly follows: "But whom say ye that I am?" (ver. 16). You have had the best opportunity to know me: what do you say? You, for three years, have been at my side and seen much of my work: what of the worker? During that time you have known my teaching: what of the teacher? Peter, the foreman of the jury, or, as Chrysostom calls him, "the leader of the apostolic choir," answered: "Thou art the Christ, the Son of the living God" (ver. 16).

Great question! Great answer! Peter is at his best. Never before or afterward does he rise to a loftier height. His vision pierces the very heavens, and his voice is the echo of Jehovah. The heart of Columbus was filled and thrilled with joy as he looked for the first time on the New World; and so was Balboa, as, from a lofty mountain crag in Panama, his eyes first saw the Pacific Ocean. Marvelous as were these discoveries, they are not to be compared with that which now burst upon the vision of Peter. It was the sun of all light, the chief of all truth, and contained within its rich bosom the incarnation, the atonement and the resurrection. It had been hid from the wise and prudent and revealed to a babe. The **proph**-ets had not all seen it clearly. To the rabbi he was a root out of the dry ground, and with no beauty that he should be desired. The eyes of the philoso-phers were "holden" so that they only saw a man —a religious enthusiast—when the Son of God stood in their midst. But Simon Peter discovered the glorious truth, and proclaimed him Lord of lords and King of kings. No wonder the Lord pronounced a blessing on him, the like of which is not to be found in all the Book: "Blessed art thou, Simon, son of Jonah: for flesh and blood hath not revealed it unto thee, but my Father which is in heaven" (ver. 17). The Psalms begin with the words, "Blessed is the man that walketh not in the counsel of the ungodly," etc., and the Sermon on the Mount with the words, "Blessed are the poor in spirit: for theirs is the kingdom of heaven." But these are benedictions on a character, while this is a blessing on an individual. And what makes this more remarkable is that we seek in vain for another called "blessed" by the lips of our Lord.

It is not strange that from this time forth he tells his disciples plainly of his death. He sees himself comprehended by, and enthroned in, the human heart, and he can safely leave the rest to his faithful followers, and he will return to the Father.

**2. Scope of the Confession** Christianity is a symmetrical system of truth, harmonious and complete, and, as such, must have a great common center. The sun is the center of the physical universe, and around him all the planets revolve. Destroy this fact, and our system of astronomy is destroyed; but accept it, and we thereby admit the laws of gravitation and attraction, the centripetal and centrifugal forces, and acknowledge that the earth and all her sister planets revolve round him, and borrow from his brightness all light and luster. Mohammedanism as a religious system has its fundamental truth, the common center which gives character to all its teachings. The truth is: Mohammed is the prophet of God. Accept this, and the whole system is accepted; reject it, and all is rejected. The confession is to Christianity what the sun is to the Copernican system of astronomy, and what the belief in Mohammed is to Mohammedanism. It is its great fundamental principle—the foundation on which the church rests—the one central truth to which all others are subordinate, and from which they receive their life and power. That this may be seen, let us analyze this confession:

a. "THOU ART THE CHRIST." Many seem to think that "Christ" is a part of the name of Jesus, and hence use the words "Jesus Christ" as they use "George Washington." But it is no part of his name. Jesus is his name, and it was divinely given (Matt. 1:20). Christ is his official title. Edward King is the name of a man. But Edward the king is much more. It means that he is the ruler of his people. Christ means anointed. The three synonymous words—"Messiah," which is Hebrew; *"Christos,"* which is Greek, and "Christ," which is English—all mean the "Anointed One," a term familiar to every Jew. So when Peter says, "Thou art the Christ," it meant that he was the "Anointed One." And they knew that but three classes of their rulers—prophets, priests and kings —were installed by anointing, and hence Jesus was declared to be their prophet, priest and king, and thus met the threefold wants of men—a power to deliver from ignorance, guilt and bondage. As Prophet he teaches, as Priest he atones and intercedes, and as King he liberates from the fetters of sin, rules over us, and leads to battle, victory and glory. He is pre-eminent. We are to hear no other prophet, to look to no other priest and to obey no other king.

*b.* "THE SON." Not a son in the sense in which all are sons; but as the Son in a peculiar sense—the divine and only Saviour.

*c.* "OF THE LIVING GOD." The besetting sin of the Jew was idolatry. Under the very shadow of Sinai, and while the Ten Commandments were still ringing in their ears, one of which specifically condemned it, they worship the golden calf. And ever afterward, till finally cured by the bitter bondage of Babylon, they were continually falling into this terrible sin; hence the significance of the phrase "the living God." He is not the son of some lifeless god, such as could be seen on every hand, but of the living God, the Maker and Preserver of all things.

That additional force and dignity may be given to this confession, let us hear a little further. God, who speaks through the Spirit, angels and men, seldom speaks in person. In the beginning he spoke, and a world sprang into existence. In Eden he spoke, and a family with language and religion was organized. After twenty-five hundred years his chariot of cloud paused over Horeb, and he spoke again, and a nation was organized. Fifteen centuries more pass by, and, as his Son comes up from his baptism in the Jordan, he again breaks the silence of the heavens and says: "This is my beloved Son, in whom I am well pleased." And a little later, on the mount of transfiguration, he repeats the same words and adds, "Hear ye him." And Paul, looking forward to the consummation of all things, says: "God hath highly exalted him, and given him a name which is above every name, that at the name of Jesus, every knee should bow, of things in heaven, and things on earth, and things under the earth, and that every tongue should confess that Jesus is Lord, to the glory of God the Father" (Phil. 2:9-11).

**3. The Confession and Baptism** It is generally conceded that in the early Church the confession was used as a test of the fitness of candidates for baptism. In Acts 8:29-39 we have, in all probability, the apostolic custom in this matter. The eunuch is convinced of the divinity of the Lord, and as they approach a suitable place for baptizing, he says, "See, here is water; what doth hinder me to be baptized? And Philip said, If thou believest with all thine heart, thou mayest. And he answered and said, I believe that Jesus

Christ is the Son of God," and immediately he **was** baptized. Admit that this clause, bringing out the confession, is an interpolation, still it is of great value. The object of the interpolator was to fill up a historic blank, so that the baptism should not appear abrupt, and, in supplying the blank, he would insert the usual custom. Now, if the interpolation harmonizes with the Scriptures, it receives all needed corroboration. We have already seen how the confession, in the early ministry of Christ, located his friends. We have also seen that, when made by Peter, it was declared to be the foundation on which the Church was to be built. The eunuch, a stranger to Philip, is asking for admission into the Church, and it is most natural that the test be applied. The confession of Timothy was evidently made in connection with his baptism. "Fight the good fight of faith, lay hold on eternal life, whereunto thou art also called, and hast confessed a good confession before many witnesses" (1 Tim. 6: 12). The two thoughts here mentioned of his call, which is by the gospel (2 Thess. 2: 14), and by laying hold on eternal life, make this clear.

The historians of the early Church corroborate this view of the confession. Irenæus (A. D. 107) speaks of the eunuch's confession, showing that the apostolic custom continued till near the close of the second century. Mosheim says that "at the first proclamation of the gospel, all that professed firmly to believe that Jesus was the only Redeemer of mankind," were baptized. Neander says: "There was only one article of faith: belief in Jesus as the Messiah." Shedd: "The candidate for admission to the Church, at his baptism, professed his faith in Christ as the Redeemer of the world." Conybeare and Howson: "In ordinary cases the sole condition required for baptism was, that the person to be baptized should acknowledge Jesus as the Messiah."

It therefore seems safe to conclude that in the early Church the confession, as we practice it to-day, was the test of the fitness for baptism. The candidate was not required to accept an elaborate creed, and his opinion regarding speculative teachings was not asked for. His acceptance or rejection depended solely on his relationship to Christ. If he confessed him as the Son of God and Saviour of men, he was baptized; if he refused to do this, he was not baptized. But later, when theology had usurped the place of the gospel, and the theologian had displaced the evangelist, other tests were added, and the primitive simplicity and power of the truth were almost destroyed.

**4. Why We Should Make the Good Confession**

a. FOR OUR OWN GOOD. It commits us publicly to Christ. It is like a brave soldier entering the territory of his foe and burning the bridges behind him. It was not a timid whisper from a cave, but a clear, round voice in the sunlight, and in the presence of men. The angels, smiling in heaven, also heard it, and the demons glaring in the pit from below. It aligns us with Christ in the face of both friends and foes. The

Christian is not to be like reeds shaken by the wind; we are not to occupy neutral territory. Travis in the Alamo, surrounded by thousands of Santa Anna's hosts floating the black flag, drew a line on the sward and said: 'Who will stand with me to the death, let him come over this side of the line." And every man went over. And Bowie, another leader, as brave as Travis. but sick, called to his companions: "Pick me up; I can not move; carry me over on that side." And how many of us have been steadied and made heroic in the after conflicts by remembering that God, angels and men had all once heard this confession from our lips? Don't fear to make a holy vow. Great men make great vows, and they serve as anchors for the soul.

*b.* FOR THE GOOD OF OTHERS. Christianity is much more than something between God and ourselves. The light must not be kept beneath the bushel. A seen religion is not always real; but a real religion is always seen. A plant grown in the dark is pale and sickly, and bears neither beautiful blossoms nor rich fruit. The bold stand taken in the confession will encourage your timid friends to confess their Saviour, as the act of Nicodemus in calling for the body of Jesus brought Joseph of Arimathea from obscurity. It will also add courage to the hosts who are battling for God, as Paul "thanked God and took courage" when he met his friends at Appii forum.

Precept is good, but example is better. It slips into the life through the eyes and ears, and finds its way down into the heart, and out into the practice, and by a secret charm, almost irresistible, it transforms life, making it beautiful and brave; or, robbing it of its virtues, leaves it wrecked and ruined on the world's highway.

*c.* FOR THE GOOD OF CHRIST. If some friend who had been true to you or to yours in some emergency were maligned on the street, your blood would boil, and you would hasten to his defense. What friend has been so true as Jesus of Nazareth? In sunshine and in shadow alike he has ever been your friend. And he has also been the friend of your mother and father. Not one single good thing received in the whole of life but that came from his gracious hands. And yet this friend is being constantly blasphemed upon our streets. And if we do not confess him, we are not neutral, bad as that would be, but we are against him. "He that is not with me is against me" (Matt. 12:30).

### REVIEW.

1. Tell us of the origin of the confession.

2. Tell of some of the great discoveries of the world.

3. What of the scope of the confession?

4. Give the meaning of the phrase "Thou art the Christ."

5. What is the meaning of the phrase "The Son"?

6. What is meant by the phrase "Of the living God"?

7. What is the relationship of baptism and the confession?

8. What good comes to the individual who makes the confession?

9. What good comes to his associates?

10. What good comes to the Lord?

# XI.
# BAPTISM

# OUTLINE—CHAPTER XI.

1. FOUR FIGURES.
    *a.* BAPTISM OF THE EARTH.
    *b.* BAPTISM OF ISRAEL IN THE SEA.
    *c.* BURIAL AND RESURRECTION.
    *d.* SUFFERINGS OF THE SAVIOUR.
2. FOUR FACTS.
    *a.* JOHN'S BAPTISM.
    *b.* BAPTISMS AT ÆNON.
    *c.* BAPTISM OF JESUS.
    *d.* BAPTISM OF THE EUNUCH.
3. FOUR OTHER PROOFS.
    *a.* DEFINITION OF "BAPTIZO."
    *b.* TESTIMONY OF THE GREEKS.
    *c.* IMMERSION SATISFIES THE SOUL.
    *d.* IT IS THE SAFE WAY.
4. APPEAL TO THE EYE.
5. DESIGN OF BAPTISM.
6. SUBJECTS OF BAPTISM.
    *a.* THE COVENANT ARGUMENT.
    *b.* BAPTISM AND CIRCUMCISION CONTRASTED.
7. HOUSEHOLD BAPTISMS.
8. OBJECTIONS TO INFANT BAPTISM.

# XI.

## BAPTISM.

The penitent soul in search of salvation, having believed on the Christ, repented of sin, and confessed the Saviour before men, is now ready to be baptized. How shall it be done? Some would answer one thing and some another, but what saith the Book? "To the law and to the testimony: if they speak not according to this word, it is because there is no light in them" (Isa. 8:20).

There is much perplexity here. Many people with honest hearts desire to do just what the Lord commands, but they do not know what it is. Having once passed through this experience, I can truly sympathize with them; and nothing will give me more pleasure than to come to their assistance in this hour of need. Let us now put away, if possible, all prejudice and preconceived notions, and study the question with the single desire of knowing the truth and walking therein. Our first inquiry is as to what is baptism.

*a.* BAPTISM OF THE EARTH.

1. Four Figures "The like figure [the overflow of the earth in the flood] whereunto even baptism doth also now save us" (1 Pet. 3:21). In Gen. 6:17-24 we are told that the flood came and the waters rose above the "high hills," "and the mountains were covered," and "every living substance

167

was destroyed from the earth." And this, to Peter, is a picture of baptism; but it can not possibly refer to anything but immersion.

*b*. BAPTISM OF ISRAEL IN THE SEA. "Moreover, brethren, I would not that you should be ignorant, how that all our fathers were under the cloud, and all passed through the sea; and were all baptized unto Moses in the cloud and in the sea" (1 Cor. 10: 1, 2). By reference to Ex. 14: 15-22, we find the facts on which this figure rests. Moses stretched out his rod "over the sea, and the waters were parted, and stood like a wall unto them on the right hand and on the left; and the children of Israel entered into the midst of the sea on dry ground," while the pillar of cloud which had led them thus far, passed over to the rear and stood between the two hosts, concealing Israel from her enemies. Paul calls this a baptism. What kind of a baptism does it represent? Certainly not affusion. It bears as little resemblance to sprinkling or pouring as does the flood. But it does resemble an immersion. As the people passed in between the walls of water, with the cloud hanging over them and in rear of them, there was a fine picture of immersion. That you may see this clearly, place two books of equal size side by side, and standing upright a few inches apart, and hang a handkerchief on them, with its folds dropping down in the rear. The books are the walls of water, and the overhanging 'kerchief is the cloud, and the Jews are concealed in the inclosure, and you have the picture.

*c.* BURIAL AND RESURRECTION. "Know ye not,
that so many of us as were baptized into Jesus
Christ were baptized into his death? Therefore
we are buried with him by baptism into death: that
like as Christ was raised up from the dead by the
glory of the Father, even so we also should walk
in newness of life. For if we have been planted
together in the likeness of his death, we shall be
also in the likeness of his resurrection" (Rom. 6:
3-5). No mistake should be made here. All are
familiar with burials. Our loved ones have left
us. We have stood by the grave, and, with break-
ing hearts and streaming eyes, have watched their
bodies sink beneath the sod. And then with the
eye of faith we have seen these bodies raised and
changed so as to be like unto the glorious body of
the Lord.

In this figure are three facts: (1) Death, (2)
burial, (3) resurrection. And so the sinner (1)
dies to sin, (2) is buried in baptism, and (3) rises
from the liquid grave to walk in newness of life.

And as we watch the penitent sinner sink
beneath the wave, and rise to go forth in the Christian life, we instinctively recognize the beauty and
perfection of the symbol. No one can fail to see
them; neither can he fail to see that the sprinkling
or pouring of a little water on the head does not
in any sense represent a burial.

*d.* SUFFERINGS OF THE SAVIOUR. "I have a
baptism to be baptized with; and how as I strait-
ened [pained] till it be accomplished!" (Luke 12:
50). The Saviour in these tender words refers to

his sufferings, and calls them a baptism. The awful agony of Gethsemane, with its bloody sweat, and Calvary, with its excruciating pain, its darkness and desertion, are before him, when from his brok· en heart would be wrung the bitter cry: "My God! my God! why hast thou forsaken me!" Let the reverent soul look upon this scene, and then ask himself, Does sprinkling a little water on the face, or the burial of the body in its depths, represent these sufferings? Surely not the former, but the latter. As we see his pure soul plunged into this bitter sea of suffering, and behold the black waves, mountain high, overflow him, we feel that nothing short of the complete burial of the body in the baptismal waters can symbolize it.

**2. Four Facts** *a.* JOHN'S BAPTISM. "In those days came John the Baptist, preaching in the wilderness of Judæa, and saying, Repent ye: for the kingdom of heaven is at hand. . . . Then went out to him Jerusalem, and all Judæa, and all the region round about Jordan, and were baptized of him in Jordan, confessing their sins" (Matt. 3:1-6). Notice that John baptized "in Jordan." He did not stand on the bank near the water, but went down into the stream. Why this? If his baptism had been by affusion, I can see no sense in it, for he could easily have dipped up the water, and saved himself and the people the inconvenience of going into it. But as it was an immersion, the going down into the river was a necessity.

*b.* BAPTIZING IN ÆNON. "And John also was

baptizing in Ænon near to Salim, because there was much water there" (John 3:23). We are not left to guess why John went to Ænon to baptize, but are told that it was "because there was much water there." Sprinkling and pouring do not require "much water," but immersion does, therefore John's baptism was immersion. If it should be said that a man located his mill at a certain place "because there was much water there," all would understand that it required "much water" to operate that mill.

*c*. BAPTISM OF JESUS. "And Jesus, when he was baptized, went up straightway out of the water" (Matt. 3:16). The Saviour's long journey to the Jordan to be baptized is finished. He makes known his mission to John, and he refuses to baptize him, claiming that himself, and not Jesus, needed to be baptized. But the Master replied: "Suffer it be so now, for thus it becometh us to fulfil all righteousness." Then John led him into the water, and buried him beneath the yielding wave, after which he "went up straightway out of the water." The Lord here fixes forever the form of this ordinance by his own baptism. As we look upon this sacred scene, let prejudice and previous bias have no place in our hearts, and let us ask, How was my Lord baptized? And when the answer is clear, let us walk in his footsteps, whatever be the cost. And what is the answer? There can be but one: He was immersed. Immersion requires coming up out of the water; sprinkling and pouring do not; therefore Jesus was immersed.

*d.* BAPTISM OF THE EUNUCH. "And as they went on their way, they came unto a certain water: and the eunuch said, See, here is water; what doth hinder me to be baptized? And Philip said, If thou believest with all thine heart, thou mayest. And he answered and said, I believe that Jesus Christ is the Son of God. And he commanded the chariot to stand still: and they went down both into the water, both Philip and the eunuch; and he baptized him. And when they were come up out of the water," etc. (Acts 8: 36-39). This story, plain enough for a primer, could not be misunderstood by men of clear heads and honest hearts. It says that they first came to the water. That would have been sufficient for affusion. No need in that case to go down into it, but only to dip it up. But it does not stop there. After coming to the water, they next go down into it, and there the baptism takes place; and after the baptism they came up out of the water. All this is necessary for immersion, but not for affusion; therefore this is a case of immersion. It is said that in the early days of our history a preacher found a bright Indian boy, told him about the Christ, gave him the New Testament, and asked him to read it and be ready to do his duty when he came again. They separated, the preacher going over his long circuit, and the boy to his wigwam to study his strange new book. After three months they met again. The preacher asked the boy if he had learned his duty to Jesus, and was told that he had. "What is it, my son?" asked the preacher. "Duty of Injun to be baptized," replied the boy. The good man thanked the Lord. The boy asked when he could be baptized, and was told to-day. He then asked where he would be baptized, and was informed that it would take place there where they were assembled. After a puzzled survey of the surroundings, in which he failed to discover any such facilities as he thought necessary, he asked, "Where is water for baptizing Injun?" "Here it is," said the preacher, pointing to a pitcher on the table. "You no put Injun down into pitcher," was the prompt reply. "I will not put you in the pitcher," said the preacher, "but will pour the water on your head." With a look of keenest disappointment, the boy turned away, saying, "You give Injun wrong book."

What a commentary on the simplicity of the language of the New Testament on the subject of baptism. This intelligent and honest-hearted boy, who had never heard of a Greek lexicon or grammar, and knew not the meaning of the word "theology," reads it without prejudice, learns that a penitent believer should be baptized, and that, in order to baptism, he has to go down into the water. And perhaps there is not, and never has been, and never will be, a similar situation without a similar conclusion.

Putting these figures and facts together, the case of immersion is made out. It is not all that could be said, but it is all that need be said. For if we will not be convinced by them, we would hardly be convinced even though a large volume was written on the subject. But that certainty may be made doubly sure, I will add

**3. Four Other Proofs**

*a.* DEFINITION OF BAPTISM. The Greek word from which we get our word "baptism" means primarily to immerse. The scholarship of the world, whatever may be the practice of these scholars as to baptism, may be regarded a unit on this point. There are two other words in the Greek, one meaning to sprinkle and the other to pour, and yet the Master passed both of them by and chose the one which means immerse. This fact alone ought forever to settle this question.

*b.* TESTIMONY OF THE GREEKS. If in China a question should be raised as to the meaning of an English word, the best way to settle it would be to appeal to the English-speaking people. Applying this principle in this case, let us appeal to the Greeks. Ancient and modern Greek is substantially the same. If the Greek Fathers—Socrates, Plato, Demosthenes and Homer—should return to Athens to-day, they would have little difficulty in reading the daily papers. It is claimed that there has been less change in the Greek language during the past twenty-four hundred years than in the English within the past five hundred years. The word "baptize" is therefore in constant use among the Greeks to-day, and it is used now as it was in the time of Christ. Cereas, a strong Greek writer, says: "Righteousness forbids a man to dip [baptize] his pen in the filth of flattery." And their religious practice is immersion. And, to cap the climax, the Presbyterians of the United States have some churches in Greece, and they practice immersion.

*c.* IMMERSION SATISFIES THE SOUL. Water slakes thirst, bread appeases hunger, light fits the eye, and sound the ear, showing that these things were designed for these purposes. And so it is with immersion. It is a well-known fact that thousands of good people are constantly becoming dissatisfied with sprinkling and pouring, and are immersed; but not so with the immersed. Their baptism satisfies the soul, and leaves it, so far as that ordinance is concerned, forever at rest, showing that as bread and water, light and sound are adapted to man's material wants, so is this ordinance adapted to his spiritual wants.

*d.* IT IS THE SAFE WAY. In material things a statement like this has wonderful weight. If the reader wished to buy a home, and, finding two places which he liked equally well, should ascertain that there was well-grounded doubt as to the title of one, but none as to the other, he would not hesitate to choose the place about whose title there was no doubt. It would not be necessary to convince him that the title was bad; only show him that it is reasonably doubtful, and he would turn from it, and he would be wise. ("The children of this world are wiser in their generation than the children of light.") And this is the exact position of the baptismal question. Immersion is not in doubt, but affusion is. The great army of those who practice nothing but immersion, and multitudes

12

of others who practice affusion, testify to the Scripturalness of immersion, and all others say it is all right, but add that they think the form of baptism is not important, and so they substitute something else for it. The title of affusion is therefore clearly in doubt; why not take the safe side?

Let us close this study with an

## 4. Appeal to the Eye

| BAPTISM REQUIRES: | IMMERSION REQUIRES: | AFFUSION REQUIRES: |
|---|---|---|
| 1. Water (Matt. 3: 16). | 1. Water. | 1. Water. |
| 2. Much water (John 3: 23.) | 2. Much water. | 2. ......... |
| 3. Coming to the water (Acts 8: 38). | 3. Coming to the water. | 3. ......... |
| 4. Going down into the water (Acts 8: 38). | 4. Going down into the water. | 4. ......... |
| 5. Coming up out of the water (Acts 8: 39). | 5. Coming up out of the water. | 5. ......... |
| 6. The figure of a burial (Rom. 6: 4). | 6. The figure of a burial. | 6. ......... |
| 7. The figure of a resurrection (Rom. 6: 4). | 7. The figure of a resurrection. | 7. ......... |

From the diagram, which is based on the Scriptures, it is seen that immersion meets the seven requirements of baptism; but affusion only meets one; therefore immersion is baptism.

**5. Design of Baptism** Baptism must have a purpose, or it would have no place in the scheme of redemption. What is that purpose? In connection with faith and repentance, the Book teaches that it is "for the remission of sins." This ought to settle the matter with Bible believers, but it does not. Many of them

believe that men are saved without baptism, and
that it has no connection with "remission of sins."
Their theory is based on a certain class of Scriptures. Let us examine this opposing theory.

"He that believeth on him is not condemned"
(John 3:18), and "he that believeth on the Son
hath everlasting life" (John 3:36), are fair samples
of the Scriptures used as a basis for this theory.
It is argued that since one is not condemned
when he believes, and as in the absence of con-
demnation he is pardoned, therefore faith is the
sole conditior of salvation.

Over against these passages let a few others be
placed. "Many other signs truly did Jesus in the
presence of his disciples which are not written in
this book; but these are written that ye might
believe that Jesus Christ is the Son of God; and
that believing ye might have life through his name"
(John 20:30). "He came unto his own, and his
own received him not, but as many as received
him, to them gave he power [or the right of
privilege] to become the sons of God" (John 1:11,
12). Here we are taught, not that the believer is
saved, but that he has the right, privilege and
power of being saved. I am not an Englishman,
but I have the right, privilege and power of becoming one if I choose. When it is declared that my
attitude to England gives me the privilege of becoming an Englishman, it is also clearly implied that I
am not an Englishman.

"Thou believest that there is one God; thou
doest well: the devils also believe, and tremble"

(Jas. 2:19). Here is faith so strong that it makes even a devil tremble, but he is not pardoned.

"Ye see then how by works [obedience] a man is justified, and not by faith only" (Jas. 2:24). This clear statement needs no comment.

The fundamental trouble with this theory is that it does not go far enough. It stops with one of the conditions of pardon. Faith is all right, but it is not the only condition of salvation. A Frenchman twenty-one years of age asks how old a man must be in this country in order to vote. You tell him twenty-one years. He hurries to the voting-place and asks for the privilege of suffrage, but is denied. Why? Not because he has not one of the qualifications of an American voter, and a most important one, but because he has only one. He must comply with all the conditions of the law of suffrage, or he can not vote. He must not scrap this law. And so we must not scrap the Scriptures on the subject of pardon. We must believe, we must repent, and we must be baptized. By scrapping the Scriptures we can prove anything. "Judas went out and hanged himself;" "Go thou and do likewise;" "What thou doest, do quickly." This is all Scripture, and, scrapped in this way, it teaches us to commit suicide, and to do it just as soon as possible.

The true theory is not that baptism alone is for the remission of sins. In fact, in the Bible sense of the term, there can be no such thing as baptism without faith, repentance, love of God, holy purposes, etc. A man without these qualifications might be buried in water a thousand times, and it would not be Bible baptism. That is the reason why we do not baptize babies. They can not exercise these spiritual qualifications which must go before and prepare the subject for baptism. Water in the abstract is absolutely without value in Christian baptism.

It is not that no one unbaptized can be saved. Infants die by the millions and go to heaven without baptism. Idiots do not need to be baptized. It is easy to conceive a penitent man so situated physically that baptism would be impossible. In that case he would be saved without it. Where there is no ability there is no responsibility. The true theory contemplates a penitent believer who can, if he will, obey the Lord in the ordinance of baptism. We note some of the proofs of this theory:

"Moreover, brethren, I would not that ye should be ignorant, how that all our fathers were under the cloud, and all passed through the sea; and were all baptized unto Moses in the cloud and in the sea" (1 Cor. 10:2). The bondage of Egypt was a type of the bondage of sin; the deliverance of Israel from this bondage by Moses was a type of the deliverance of the world from the bondage of sin; Moses as a leader was a type of Jesus Christ; and baptism into Moses was typical of baptism into Christ. When, then, were the Israelites made free? Not when they began their march from Egypt; and not when they halted in front of the sea. The hosts of Pharaoh are close upon them, and all are filled with fear. But soon the sea is opened, and, obeying the command of their leader, they passed through it—are baptized unto Moses—and on the other side they realize their freedom, and sing the song of deliverance. And so when we forsake sin, and, in full assurance of faith, are baptized "into Christ," we are pardoned and made free men in the Lord. But our freedom, as in the case of Israel, does not precede, but follows, our baptism.

"The like figure whereunto even baptism doth also now save us (not the putting away of the filth of the flesh, but the answer of a good conscience toward God,) by the resurrection of Jesus Christ" (1 Pet. 3: 21). Noah's salvation was from destruction by the waters of the flood. He did what God told him to do—prepared an ark—and Jehovah brought him safely through the waters, and on this side of them he rejoiced in salvation. And thus, Peter tells us that baptism saves us. But, lest we make a mistake, he says our baptism is not "the putting away of the filth of the flesh," as were the ceremonial dippings of the old covenant, "but the answer of a good conscience toward God." How "the answer of a good conscience"? The penitent man who is well taught knows that the Saviour says, "He that believeth and is baptized shall be saved," and his conscience will never cease to chide so long as this known duty is neglected.

"John did baptize in the wilderness, and preach the baptism of repentance for the remission of sins" (Mark 1:4). "The baptism of repentance" is one

which grows out of repentance; is produced because
one is penitent; and such a baptism is for remission
of sins. It is not baptism by itself, but baptism in
connection with repentance.

"Except a man be born of water and of the
Spirit, he cannot enter into the kingdom of God"
(John 3:5). Our sins are forgiven when we
enter the kingdom of God; but the birth of water
(baptism) and of the Spirit lies between us and
that kingdom, therefore this birth is for remission
of sins.

"As many of you as have been baptized into
Christ have put on Christ" (Gal. 3:27). Out of
Christ we are unsaved; in Christ we are saved;
whatever, therefore, puts us in Christ is essential
to salvation; baptism does this, hence it is for the
remission of sins.

"Not by works of righteousness which we have
done, but according to his mercy he saved us by
the washing of regeneration and renewing of the
Holy Spirit" (Tit. 3:5). We are saved by the
washing of regeneration; the washing of regeneration means baptism; therefore baptism is for the
remission of sins.

"Go ye into all the world and preach the gospel to every creature; he that believeth and is baptized shall be saved; but he that believeth not
shall be damned" (Mark 16:15, 16). This passage
is of special importance, because it is the commission under which salvation is to be offered to the
world. And we should rejoice that its terms are so
simple that all can understand them. The gospel

is to be preached; those who believe it and are baptized shall be saved; therefore baptism is necessary to salvation. It may be suggested that it only says that "he that believeth not shall be damned," not he that believeth not and is not baptized. That is true. The unbeliever will be lost, whether baptized or not. As already shown, there can be no baptism without faith. The man who loves a good woman and is married is happy, but the man who loves not is miserable. This is true of him, whether married or not, hence the phrase "and is married" need not be repeated in order to describe his condition. There can be no true marriage without love, and there can be no Bible baptism without faith, hence the awful truth that the unbeliever is lost, and the man who loves not is not happy.

"Men and brethren, what shall we do? Then Peter said unto them, Repent, and be baptized every one of you in the name of Jesus Christ for the remission of sins, and ye shall receive the gift of the Holy Spirit" (Acts 2: 37, 38). This Scripture is also of special importance because it is a part of the first sermon preached under the commission of our Lord, and it was preached by a man supernaturally guided, so that a mistake was impossible. The language is as simple as the world ever heard. The audience was convinced of the crime of murdering Jesus of Nazareth, the Son of God, and in their desperation they cried out to know what they should do. The answer is, "Repent, and be baptized." But that is not all. This was to be done "in the name of Jesus Christ," this man

whom ye have murdered. And this is not all. He
next tells them the purpose of this repentance and
baptism: it is for the "remission of sins." And
even this is not all: and he connects with it the
promise of the indwelling Spirit: "And ye shall
receive the gift of the Holy Spirit."

We must hear J. S. Sweeney on this passage.
"Does this language of Peter make baptism a condition precedent to remission of sins? We say it
does, and here we will stand or fall. The controversy hinges on the meaning of the word 'for.' We
say it means 'in order to,' while it is contended by
our opponents that its sense is 'because of.' It will
be granted that it sometimes has the meaning we
give it in this case; and we are ready to admit that
it sometimes means 'because of.' And what is here
said of 'for' may be truly said of the Greek word
it represents. Then, can we ascertain what the
word means in this passage? Happily for the
truth, there is a circumstance in the case which
enables us to determine this question. It is this:
The relation which 'for' expresses here between
baptism and remission, is the same that repentance
sustains to remission, the relation of both to remission being expressed at once by the same word;
therefore that relation is one. The law to the
believer is, 'Repent, and be baptized for the remission of sins!' Will any one say that we may read,
'Repent, and be baptized because of the remission
of sins'? Does any one believe in repentance because of the remission of sins? Not one so believes.
The relation of repentance to remission is that of

a precedent to a subsequent. But the relation of baptism must be the same, for it is expressed by the same word, and at the same time; therefore the relation of baptism to the remission of sins is that of a precedent to a consequent."

"And now why tarriest thou? Arise, and be baptized, and wash away thy sins, calling on the name of the Lord" (Acts 22:16). Saul, the mighty persecutor, was still in his sins; he was told to wash them away (figuratively, of course) in baptism; therefore baptism is for the remission of sins.

Let us obey the whole law of pardon, lest the fate of Eden fall upon us. A false teacher entered the beautiful garden, and told Adam and Eve that it was not necessary to do all God said. Most likely he told them that the clause prohibiting the eating of fruit from a certain tree was arbitrary, unreasonable and unphilosophic. They heeded his voice, and disregarded a plain command; not plainer, however, than baptism is to us, and they fell, and brought death into the world with all its woe. May this warning make us wise.

**6. Subjects of Baptism** Having found that the baptism of the Bible is immersion, and that it is for the remission of sins, we next ask, Who should be baptized? There are two answers to this question: (1) Penitent believers, and (2) infants not old enough to believe. Those giving the second answer, of course, do not oppose the baptism of believers. In fact, the baptism of penitent believers, like immersion, is not in controversy. It is common ground. Only the second answer is in debate, and to its discussion we now proceed.

The identity of the covenants is the first argument generally used in support of infant baptism. It is claimed that the covenants of the Old and New Testaments are the same, and that as there were infants in the first, there are also infants in the second. Dr. McLean, speaking of the day of Pentecost, says· "'The language is such as would be used of the continuance of the Old Testament church. . . . This church was now changed from a Jewish to the Christian church." In reply to this let it be said:

*a.* THERE WAS NO TRUE CHURCH DURING THE OLD TESTAMENT TIMES. The people of Israel in the wilderness were not the church in the Christian sense of the term, but only in the sense that they were called out from Egypt and made a separate body. The conditions of membership did not involve piety, change of heart, etc. They were not required to be born again (John 3:5) as in the Christian church. They were in a large measure idolaters. It would be much more in harmony with the facts to call them, not a church, but the commonwealth of Israel, a semi-religious institution into which men could enter and remain without spiritual requirements. Infants were in that commonwealth just as they are in the commonwealth of Texas.

It is a very significant fact that the King James translators do not give us the word "church" in the whole of the Old Testament; and not in the New until the sixteenth chapter of Matthew. This shows that they were unwilling to identify anything found in Israel with the New Testament idea of the church.

*b.* THE CHURCH HAD NOT BEEN BUILT DURING THE PERSONAL MINISTRY OF CHRIST. "But whom say ye that I am? And Simon Peter answered and said, Thou art the Christ, the Son of the living God. And Jesus answered, and said unto him, Blessed art thou, Simon Bar-jona, for flesh and blood hath not revealed it unto thee, but my Father who is in heaven. And I say also unto thee, that thou art Peter, and upon this rock [your confession] I will build my church" (Matt. 16: 15-18). This is fifteen hundred years after the Israelites had been called out of Egypt, and still the church is a thing of the future. According to this theory, it was then old—fifteen centuries old; but according to the facts as gleaned from the Saviour, it was still to be built. Suppose the reader should say to a friend, as he pointed to a foundation, "On this foundation I will build my house," would it be reasonable to understand him to mean that he would remodel an old house already built? Certainly not. And yet this language is not stronger than the language of the Saviour.

*c.* DIFFERENCES BETWEEN THE COVENANTS. "Behold, the days come, saith the Lord, that I will make a new covenant with the house of Israel, and with the house of Judah; not according to the covenant that I made with their fathers in the day

that I took them by the hand to bring them out of
the land of Egypt; which covenant they brake,
although I was an husband unto them, saith the
Lord. But this shall be the covenant that I will
make with the house of Israel· After those days,
saith the Lord, I will put my law in their inward
parts, and write it in their hearts; and will be
their God, and they shall be my people. And they
shall teach no more every man his neighbor, and
every man his brother, saying, Know the Lord: for
they shall all know me, from the least of them unto
the greatest of them, for I will forgive their
iniquity, and I will remember their sin no more"
(Jer. 31: 31-34).

Here is a promise six hundred years before
Christ that "a new covenant" would be made.
Turning to the eighth chapter of Hebrews, we find
that the promise was fulfilled. "In that he saith,
A new covenant, he hath made the first old. Now
that which decayeth and waxeth old is ready to
vanish away." Such language would not be used
in connection with the "continuance of the Old
Testament church." It is a "new covenant"—not
a renewed one—which was promised and given.
Let us note the points of difference:

(1) Only male children were circumcised (Gen.
17: 10); but both sexes were baptized.

(2) They were circumcised when eight days old
(Gen. 17: 12); but no particular age is observed
in infant baptism.

(3) If uncircumcised, the child was "cut off
from his people" (Gen. 17: 14), but in the new

covenant Paul says, "If ye be circumcised, Christ shall profit you nothing" (Gal. 5:2).

(4) If baptism has taken the place of circumcision, it is strange that the famous Jerusalem council (Acts 15) did not so declare. The matter was before them, for in their decision, which was scattered broadcast among the churches, it is said: "Forasmuch as we have heard that certain which went out from us have troubled you, saying, Ye must be circumcised and keep the law," etc. (ver. 24). How easy and natural for them, if such was the case, to have settled this troublesome matter for all time by saying that baptism in the new covenant takes the place of circumcision in the old. But they did not say it, and that proves, with the force of a demonstration, that it is not true.

(5) What, then, is true? "He is not a Jew which is one outwardly; neither is that circumcision which is outward in the flesh; but he is a Jew who is one inwardly; and circumcision is that of the heart, in the spirit, and not in the letter; whose praise is not of men, but of God" (Rom. 2:28, 29). The circumcision of the old covenant was of the flesh, but that of the new is of the heart, and hence we have both it and baptism in the new; the one using the blood of Christ and the other the baptismal waters; the one pertaining to the heart and the other to the flesh.

**7. Household Baptisms**

This argument for infant baptism was so completely overturned by L. B. Wilkes in the "Louisville Debate" that I give it to the reader:

"To demonstrate infant baptism from household baptism, my friend must adopt and defend the two following syllogisms: All households have infants in them; the apostles baptized some households; therefore the apostles baptized infants.

"Now observe, if the major premise is not true, that all households have infants in them, households might have been baptized, and yet no infants baptized. The minor premise is true, that the apostles baptized some households; but it does not follow, since the major premise is known to be false, that infants were baptized. The major premise must be true, and the minor must be true, else the conclusion sought to be arrived at does not follow. Yet the conclusion is precisely what my friend is compelled to prove, or what he has under-taken to prove.

"His statement is that infant baptism is author-ized by the word of God. This will require another syllogism, growing out of the previous one; viz., if the apostles baptized any infants, then infant baptism is authorized by the word of God. The apostles did baptize some infants; therefore infant baptism is authorized by the word of God. The minor premise states that they did baptize some infants, and the conclusion is that, therefore, infant baptism is authorized by the word of God. But, in order to reach this conclusion, it must be shown that there are infants in all households, which we know is not true. If there were infants in all households, then by proving that the apostles bap-tized households, it would follow that they baptized infants; but since we know that there are house-holds with no infants in them, it does not follow that the apostles baptized infants from the fact that they baptized households.''

This logic is conclusive, and the case might rest here; but we will corroborate it by an examination of some of these households. In the household of Cornelius (Acts 10: 46) they heard, they spoke with tongues, and they magnified God; hence there were no infants there. In the household of Lydia (Acts 16: 14, 40) all were old enough to be comforted by the words of the apostle; hence there were no infants there. In the case of the jailer (Acts 16: 34) all rejoiced and believed; hence there were no infants there. In the case of Crispus (Acts 18: 8) all believed; hence there were no infants there. And in the case of Stephanas (1 Cor. 1: 16; 16: 15) they "addicted [gave] themselves to the min-istry;" hence there were no infants there. And so of the other households.

Let us close this refutation by an appeal to modern experience. An Illinois preacher has bap-tized three households of jailers in which there were no infants. Another has baptized ten house-holds, and yet he never baptized an infant. And doubtless hundreds of my readers have had much the same experience.

**8. Objections to Infant Baptism**    *a.* IT REVERSES THE DIVINE ORDER. "When therefore the Lord knew how the Pharisees had heard that Jesus made and baptized more dis-ciples," etc. (John 4: 1). "Go ye therefore and

teach [make disciples] all nations, baptizing them,"
etc. (Matt. 28:19). These Scriptures show that
the order of the Saviour in his work, and the
order to be followed by the apostles in theirs, was
to teach first, and then baptize the taught. The
commission, according to the theory of infant baptism, should read, "Go ye therefore and baptize all
nations, and then teach them," etc.

*b*. IT OBLITERATES THE DISTINCTION BETWEEN
THE CHURCH AND THE WORLD. If infant baptism,
from this day, should become universal, and should
so continue for a single generation, every infant
having been baptized, the church and the world
would be one, and the spiritual distinction which
God desires to exist between them would be blotted
out.

*c*. IT DOES NO GOOD. What does a child gain
by being baptized which it might not gain without
baptism? What does it lose without baptism that
it might not lose with it? What is either gained
or lost in time or eternity by having the child baptized, or by a failure to have it baptized? Whether
baptized or not, it is saved; hence its baptism is
meaningless and profitless. Two little children,
pure as when God gave them to the earth, are
sleeping side by side in the cemetery; one was baptized, and the other was not. What difference did
it make in this life? and what difference will it
make in the life beyond?

*d*. IT IGNORES THE POWER OF CHOICE. This is
one of our royal privileges. We are not machines,
driven or dragged hither and thither according to

13

the whims and caprices of another; but we are **men** made in the image of God, and endowed with the power of saying "'Yes" or "No" even to our Maker. But infant baptism ignores this high prerogative, and the child is baptized whether it wills or not, and generally much against its will. Suppose a young man should attend a series of meetings, but would not become a Christian. After much teaching, preaching and exhortation have failed, a number of his friends seize him, and, against his most earnest protest, baptize him. Every one would call this an outrage, and such it would be. But how much worse to baptize against his will one who weighs 150 pounds, or one of half that weight? You answer that the cases are the same. Well, how much worse to baptize one of seventy-five pounds against his will than one of 100 pounds? The answer is that they are both equally bad. Then, if it is wrong to baptize one of 100 pounds against his will, how can it be right to baptize one of ten pounds?

### Review.

1. Give four figures in proof of immersion.
2. Give four facts in proof of immersion.
3. Give four other proofs of immersion.
4. Give the diagram argument.
5. State the false theory as to the design of baptism.
6. What is the true theory on this question?
7. Give some proofs of this theory.
8. Give J. S. Sweeney's argument.

9. What is the covenant argument for infant baptism?

10. Answer this argument.

11. Give L. B. Wilkes' argument on household baptisms.

12. State the objections to infant baptism.

# XII.
# EVIDENCE OF PARDON

# OUTLINE—CHAPTER XII.

1. CHARACTER AND METHOD OF WITNESSES.
   a. GOD'S SPIRIT.
   b. MAN'S SPIRIT.
2. WHAT IS THE TESTIMONY?
   a. NOT A NEW REVELATION.
   b. NOT FEELINGS.
   c. NOT SINCERITY.
   d. BUT THE JOINT TESTIMONY OF GOD AND MAN.
3. A PICTURE.

# XII.

## Evidence of Pardon.

When a child does wrong, sees his error, repents, and asks his father's forgiveness, can he not, and should he not, know whether he has been forgiven? It would seem that a good father would so speak to his penitent boy as not to leave him in doubt. And will our Father in heaven do less? Surely not. And therefore I believe that when we repent of our sins, and turn to him for forgiveness, he will speak to us in words so simple and clear that we may know we have been pardoned.

This conclusion is reached in another way: God wants us to be happy; but this can not be without a knowledge of forgiveness; therefore, he will furnish us that knowledge. Should this penitent boy be in doubt as to his forgiveness, to the extent of that doubt he would be unhappy. Hear his sad soliloquy: "At times I think father has forgiven me, and often I doubt, hence my joy fluctuates with every phase of hope. Oh that I had something solid on which to rest this hope!" And when he sings, his favorite song will be the one which I used to sing when groping in darkness and doubt at this very point:

"'Tis a point I long to know,
And oft it causes anxious thought:
Do I love the Lord or no?
Am I his or am I not?"

There have been thousands of people in the past, and there are thousands to-day, who have been faithful, or are now faithful in their service of God, and yet they never had comfort at this point.

An additional proof of this point is found in the New Testament teachings, where all is the most confident assurance. "We are always *confident,* knowing that while we are at home in the body, we are absent from the Lord" (2 Cor. 5:6). "Being then *made free* from sin, ye become the servants of righteousness" (Rom. 6:18). "In whom we *have redemption* through his blood, the forgiveness of sins" (Eph. 1:7). *"Knowing,* brethren beloved, your election of God" (1 Thess. 1:4). "Wherefore the rather, brethren, give diligence to make your calling and election *sure"* (2 Pet. 1:10). "Hereby we do *know* that we know him, if we keep his commandments" (1 John 2:3). "Beloved, now *are we the sons of God,* and it doth not yet appear what we shall be: but we know that when he shall appear, we shall be like him; for we shall see him as he is" (1 John 3:2). "We *know that we have passed from death unto life,* because we love the brethren" (1 John 3:14). Not a single note of doubt or uncertainty here, but all the language of confidence.

But how may we secure this knowledge and enjoy this assurance? In order to do this, let it be remembered that this is not a question of dreams or fleshly sensations, but one of fact, and as such it must be settled by testimony. And Paul furnishes the key to the problem in these words: "The Spirit itself beareth witness with our spirit, that we are the children of God" (Rom. 8:16). Note the fact that there are two witnesses, and not one, as many suppose. God's Spirit does not testify to our spirit, but the two spirits testify jointly. If I testify to you, there is but one witness; but if I testify with you, there are two.

1. Character and Method of the Witnesses

*a.* GOD'S SPIRIT. When the lawyer shows that the witnesses against his client are not reliable, his case is safe, regardless of their testimony. But if this can not be done, and the testimony is conclusive, the case is lost. Let the same rule apply here; and in its application we ask: (1) Is the witness trustworthy? and (2) How does he testify?

Applied to God's Spirit, the first question can not be discussed. His is the Spirit of truth, the fountain of all spiritual knowledge, and hence it can not be doubted. We therefore raise the second question, How does he testify? "But when they deliver you up, take no thought how or what ye shall speak; for it shall be given you in that same hour what ye shall speak, for it is not ye that speak, but the Spirit of your Father which speaketh in you" (Matt. 10:18-20). This teaches that the Spirit testifies through words.

"Which things also we speak, not in the words which man's wisdom teacheth, but which the Holy Spirit teacheth" (1 Cor. 2:13, 14). Here, again, this witness testifies in words. Having ascertained that the first witness is reliable, and that he **testifies** through words, we next inquire as to

*b.* MAN'S SPIRIT. Possibly some reader questions the fact that man's spirit witnesses to himself. Let us hear Paul again: "I say the truth in Christ, I lie not, my conscience also bearing me witness in the Holy Spirit" (Rom. 9:1). The same verb is used here as in Rom. 1:16. Is this witness also reliable? Can we rest confidently on this testimony as on the other? A man murdered his wife. Suborned witnesses, skillfully instructed by a shrewd lawyer, proved that he was forty miles from her at the time of the murder, and was therefore innocent. But the spirit of the man knew the testimony was false, and that he was guilty. And if the angels and the redeemed had corroborated the false witnesses, the spirit of the man would still have remained the same. And, upon the other hand, if the husband had been innocent, no amount of testimony could have convinced his spirit of guilt. This great question did not depend on outside testimony. And thus it is seen that the spirit of man is trustworthy.

A word of caution: I do not mean to say that one may not do wrong, and still have his spirit encourage him in the wrong. This will be cleared a little later. I only mean to teach that his spirit's testimony is always in harmony with the facts as it knows them. If a child knows nothing but affusion as baptism, its spirit will testify in favor of affusion. But let the facts be fully given, and it will declare for immersion. Is not this the highest type of a witness?

How does this witness testify? Like God's Spirit, it testifies through words, or their equivalents. A man is before a jury. He knows all the facts in the case pending. But he refuses to speak in answer to the questions of counsel and court. How long will it require to ascertain the testimony of his spirit? It can never be known until he chooses to coin it into words.

Two important questions are now settled; viz., both of our witnesses are absolutely reliable, and both testify, not through fleshly sensations, dreams, etc., but through words. Well may we tremble if the testimony is against us; and well may we rejoice if it be in our favor.

**2. What Is This Testimony?**
*a.* IT IS NOT A NEW REVELATION. Many expect Christ to speak to them to-day as he did to the timid woman who touched his garment (Matt. 9:20), saying, "Thy faith hath made thee whole;" or to the palsied penitent (Mark 2:5), saying, "Son, thy sins be forgiven thee;" or to the dying thief (Luke 23:43), saying, "To-day thou shalt be with me in paradise." The written word as found in the Bible is not enough. They expect the still small voice to make a new revelation to them. They seem never to have read these plain words: "According as his divine power *hath given* unto us all things that pertain unto life and godliness," etc. (2 Pet. 1:3). Notice the time of the verb—"hath given;" not, "will give." Almost two thousand years ago "all things" pertaining unto life and godliness had been given; the forgiveness of sins per-

tains unto "life and godliness"; therefore all things on the subject have already been given. Why expect a new revelation? It is as unreasonable as to expect a special telegram to confirm a well-attested letter from a friend. If you will not believe his letter, what evidence has he that you will believe his telegram? If we will not believe the word of God in the Bible, why would we believe a special message from the same source?

*b.* It Is Not Our Feelings. Multitudes rest this great matter on the frail basis of fleshly feelings. If they feel good, they are forgiven; if they feel bad, they are not forgiven. They forget the feelings are largely dependent on health, the weather, our surroundings, etc. But salvation is independent of all these. We may be saved in health or in sickness; in good weather or bad; and in spite of surroundings. They forget, also, that feelings are deceptive. As Jacob listened to the false reports of his sinful boys, and looked upon the bloody coat of Joseph, he felt that his child was dead. But his feelings deceived him. They seem not to understand that feelings are an effect, and not a cause. God forgives. This is a cause. The forgiven soul is happy. This is the result. We do not know we are forgiven because we are happy, but we are happy because we know we are forgiven. But let no one conclude that we ignore, or even place a light estimate on, feelings. A religion that does not make one feel happy is a false religion. When God forgives, every emotion of the soul leaps for joy, and the lips sing the praises of Jehovah.

*c.* IT IS NOT OUR SINCERITY. Jacob was sincere when he said his boy was dead, and that he would see him no more this side the grave. Paul was as sincere when persecuting the church as he was, later, when he defended it, and gave his life as a sacrifice for Christ. Can you not recall cases in your own life, and in the lives of your friends, in which you were sincerely in the wrong? This fine element of character—sincerity—is found alike in the bosoms of those whose causes are just, and those whose causes are unjust, and hence it proves only the moral integrity of the man, and not the righteousness of his cause.

A cruel illustration of this thought took place recently in one of our State prisons. The boy was not very bright, and some of his fellow-prisoners brought him what he thought was a regular pardon from the Governor. He believed it was genuine, and he leaped and danced for joy, and stood at the door watching for an officer to come and lead him out. He was happy as if it had been true, but his happiness did not last. His feelings deceived him.

If the evidence of pardon is not in a new revelation, and not in feelings, and not in sincerity, what is it?

*d.* IT IS THE JOINT TESTIMONY OF THESE TWO WITNESSES. One points out the way to pardon, and the other assures us that we have walked in that way. God's Spirit says we must believe, which changes the heart; and man's spirit says we must repent, which changes the life; and man's spirit says he has repented. God's Spirit says we must be baptized, which changes the state or relationship; and man's spirit says he has been baptized. And when changed in heart, life and relationship, he is "a new creature in Christ Jesus."

Now that we have this vital point made clear as sunlight, imagine an honest and intelligent Christian testing himself. He looks within and asks himself if he has believed; and the answer is instantaneous, and without one vestige of doubt, that he does believe. There is no more doubt on this point than there is as to his existence. He knows that he is a believer. Looking within again, he asks himself as to his repentance; and the answer is as prompt and as free from doubt as before, that he has repented. With equal certainty he inquires as to his baptism, and thus the entire question is settled. To doubt now is either to question his own consciousness, or to disbelieve the word of God. And while reason reigns and rules he can not do the former, and until he becomes an infidel, he can not do the latter.

3. A Picture    A man is in the penitentiary. His friends petition the Governor, and he is pardoned on certain conditions. With a happy heart he starts to his home. The sheriff of his county, not knowing of his pardon, meets him on the highway, and commands him to halt. "Why do you halt me?" says the man; "I have been pardoned." "What evidence can you give of your pardon?" answers the sheriff. "Well, Mr. Sheriff," says the man, "it is a strange story I have to tell,

but it is true. Last night about twelve o'clock, when all was dark and still in my cell, suddenly a light brighter than yonder sun shone about me, and I heard a voice saying, 'John Smith, you are a pardoned man.'" The sheriff coolly responds: "I've no doubt you think you saw and heard all this, and doubtless it would be all right in religious circles, but it is a little too fanciful for the courts of Cæsar, and you may consider yourself under arrest." But the man, laying his hand on his heart, continues: "Mr. Sheriff, I feel that I am pardoned." "I do not question your feelings," answers the sensible but not oversentimental sheriff, "but feelings, like visions and voices, are not good evidence in our courts," and he is about to proceed with his prisoner to the jail. "Hold, Mr. Sheriff!" cries the man with much vehemence, "I declare to you that I am thoroughly honest and sincere!" "That may be true," replies the officer, "but, like everything else you've said, it is unsatisfactory as evidence in our courts, and therefore it is my duty to arrest you;" and his stern face indicates business; when the ex-convict pulls from his pocket a paper, saying: "Here is evidence which I know you will accept." And it proves to be a pardon from Governor Colquitt, of Texas, bearing the seal of the State, in which the man is pardoned provided that on or before 1 P. M. of December 1, 1913, he leave the State and never returns. "This is all right," says the sheriff. "Why did you not show it at first and save all this trouble?"

At 12:30 P. M., December 1, he crosses the Rio

Grande River at El Paso, and takes up his abode in Mexico. You meet him an hour later, and ask him if he has been pardoned. What would he say? Would he answer that he thought so? he hoped so? he felt so? Certainly not. His answer would be prompt, clear and positive. He would say, "Yes."

And then, if you should ask for the evidence on which he based this confident answer, he would tell you that Governor Colquitt promised his pardon on certain conditions, and that he had complied with those conditions. The spirit of the Governor, the pardoning power, had named the conditions of pardon, and the spirit of the man assured him that he had faithfully observed them; and therefore he had the highest posible evidence of forgiveness. Let the Governor represent God, and the pardoned man the sinner, and we have not only a true picture of this most important principle, but one so simple that all can understand.

## REVIEW.

1. Does God desire our happiness?
2. How many witnesses testify in our study?
3. How do they testify?
4. Give the negative side of the answer.
5. Give the positive side of the answer.
6. Illustrate the whole question.

THE END.

CPSIA information can be obtained
at www.ICGtesting.com
Printed in the USA
BVHW04*0746280818
525723BV00019B/102/P